THE
ADVENTURES
OF HOMER
FINK

BY SIDNEY OFFIT

SCHOLASTIC BOOK SERVICES

NEW YORK • TORONTO • LONDON • AUCKLAND • SYDNEY • TOKYO

The author wishes to thank the New York Public Library for the use of the Frederick Lewis Allen Memorial Room, where this story was written and other lines read.

To the memory of Arnold Ortman, teacher, coach and friend of the students of the former Lafayette Junior High School, Baltimore, Maryland . . .
And . . .
   To the school boys and girls of Public School 6, Manhattan, who first encouraged the tales of Homer Fink.

Copyright © 1966 by Sidney Offit. Illustrations copyright © 1966 by St. Martin's Press, Inc. This edition is published by Scholastic Book Services, a division of Scholastic Magazines, Inc., by arrangement with St. Martin's Press, Inc.

4th printing . . . . February 1973

Printed in the U.S.A.

1

IT STARTED when the loud-speaker conked out. I don't suppose it would have been important if any other boy or girl at Junior High School 79 had been speaking. Most kids around our age aren't Einsteins, but they can figure out that if you are speaking to eight hundred students and the teachers, and the loud-speaker dies, the best thing to do is close your mouth and wait. But it wasn't any other student. It was my friend, Homer Fink. And Homer is an Einstein.

That's what the other kids in our class call him. They call him another name too, particularly when he's the only one in class who has the answers to the teacher's questions.

They say it fast, three times in a row: "Fink. Fink. Fink."

Homer usually smiles and touches his thumb and index finger like an "O" for onward.

I asked him about this once and Homer said, "Fink employed as a noun other than a proper name refers to an informer—a squealer. In the lexicon of the labor unions a fink is a strike-breaker. It may also mean one who visits a carnival not to spend but to find cause for complaint to police." Then he paused, waiting for it to sink in, but it didn't. When Homer talks like that I don't even try to understand what he says. Most of the time I get the feeling that he's remembered something from our homework that I've forgotten. Usually I just shrug and say, "I guess so."

That's what I did after he told me about "fink."

"So you can see that the usage in this instance it irrelevant," Homer went on. "My information was enlightening, not conspiratorial."

Homer doesn't talk like that to impress people. That's the way he is. I guess he was born that way.

We have an oratory contest at school every year. The winner gets a dictionary, which isn't much, but the teacher always tells us that the big thing is the "honor."

By the time you reach the ninth grade you

know without even going to the assembly that you're in for "Gunga Din," "The Wreck of the Hesperus," Lincoln's Gettysburg Address and "Give Me Liberty or Give Me Death."

Each homeroom picks its two best speakers. We knew in our class that Phillip Moore was going to make it. He's definitely the boy you'd want on your side in war or peace or a pick-up game of touch football in the yard after school.

Phillip recited "If," a poem by Rudyard Kipling. His expression was so serious it almost made me want to cry. (Laura Epps did cry, but that doesn't count because Laura cries at all kinds of things such as hearing about how Lou Gehrig died—and she can't even play baseball.)

Homer was looking out the window when the teacher called on him. Homer Fink is always looking out windows or studying the floor or looking off at the sky as if he sees something there. Most of the time the teacher has to say his name two or three times to get his attention. But Miss Pierce—she's our homeroom teacher—is very patient. She repeated, "Homer—Homer Fink. May I have your attention, Homer?"

There was a chorus of "Fink, Fink, Fink."

This happens lots of times, which is probably just as well because if Homer really did listen and knew what was going on in class all the time he would have all the right answers and we'd hear more of the other, "Fink. Fink. Fink." No matter what Homer says or how he explains it, the chorus makes me feel very uncomfortable.

Well, on the day of the oratory tryouts, Homer heard the class repeat his name. He turned his head slowly and blinked his eyes and said very softly, "Yes, ma'am—in the third millennium B.C., equinoxes and solstices were determined in China by means of culminating stars."

The class cracked up. Brian Spitzer roared and banged on his desk and Trudy Deal tried so hard to control her laugh, it came out a great big raspberry—brrrrrr.

"Now . . . now, childen." Miss Pierce clapped her hands and nodded her head in a way she has of letting us know it's all right to laugh a little but that it's time to stop. "Thank you very much, Homer. It's good of you to bring us this information about astronomy, but we were discussing the stars last Wednesday, and next week when we talk about them again we'll be looking forward to hearing what you have learned."

Homer jumped to his feet.

"No genuine science of astronomy was founded until the Greeks translated experience into theory," he went on. "Among the astronomers of antiquity Hipparchus and Ptolemy were the greatest." Homer was off and running now, and

6

there was no stopping him. He knew these things and he wanted to tell us all about them. I don't suppose it ever occurred to Homer Fink that other kids weren't as concerned about learning as he was. To tell the truth, I'm not interested in half the things Homer knows about. But I listen because sometimes Homer gets hot on a subject like the Second World War. I remember one afternoon he charted the battles of Coral Sea and Midway for me. Homer really had me believing he was right there with Admiral William Halsey. When Homer described how the *Lexington* went down, I started treading water to save my life.

But that was the story of a battle, and this time Homer was going on about charting the path of Jupiter.

"We know that the orbital period of Jupiter is nearly twelve years," said Homer and he started to the blackboard.

He would have made it too and gone on drawing the pictures if he hadn't tripped on his shoelace. Homer may know all about the stars and the battles of World War II but he never did learn how to make a bowknot.

Phillip Moore caught Homer and broke his fall. Phillip Moore is in great condition.

"Take it easy, Homer—calm down," I heard Phillip say. "You'll break your neck."

"Yes—well, thank you," said Homer.

The class started to laugh again and Miss Pierce made a short speech about laughing with people and not at them. She told us that not all people were alike and while it may be true that Homer Fink was sometimes different, he had feelings like the rest of us and it was impolite to laugh at another person's misfortune. Then she complimented Homer for knowing so much about astronomy and promised him that the next time we had a free period she would be certain to let him chart the orbit of the planet Jupiter. We all knew that wouldn't work because one thing for sure, Homer never talked about the same thing twice. Then Miss Pierce suggested that Homer tie his shoelace.

Homer bent down and flipped the strings around. I was sitting in the middle of the room —so I bent forward to see how he was making out. With most kids who are in junior high school, you wouldn't think twice about their tying their shoelaces. But with Homer Fink you never could tell; I had untied really fantastic knots for him lots of times. He didn't get to tying his shoelaces often, but when he did he went at it so hard you'd think he was locking the door to Fort Knox. I followed the knot as closely as I could.

"And now, Homer, we'd like to hear your recitation," Miss Pierce said. "Introduce yourself, identify your source, and conduct yourself

8

exactly as you will if the class selects you to represent us in the oratory contest in front of the entire school."

"My name is Homer Fink," Homer began. "My homeroom is 9-1, and I am going to recite 'Potpourri' from the selections of that class."

Trudy Deal snickered and Phillip Moore glared at her from his seat. In addition to being best at everything, Phillip Moore is a good sport.

> Listen, my children, and you shall hear
> Of the midnight ride of Paul Revere, . . .

There was a look on Homer's face that I recognized. Homer is a redhead and he really lives up to the saying that redheads are hotheads. But usually when Homer is angry he stamps and swings his arms in the air and curses in all the languages he knows. He'll do this for a couple of minutes, and while it is going on you'd swear he's going to burst, or break down a wall, or take off and start flying. But this wasn't that kind of anger. It was as if Homer was boiling underneath but couldn't explode and had to let his anger out in short insults.

The class settled down to hearing about Paul Revere again, even though Brian Spitzer had recited it earlier and Homer had called it by some other name. (Latin we guessed.)

9

> Half a league, half a league,
>   Half a league onward,
> All in the valley of Death
>   Rode the six hundred.

Paul Revere's ride was getting bloodier, and then Homer told us:

> The uniform 'e wore
> Was nothin' much before,
> An' rather less than 'arf o' that be'ind . . .
> It was "Din! Din! Din!
> You 'eathen, where the mischief 'ave you
>   been?"

Homer went on like that, reciting bits of all the poems and speeches we'd heard all morning. He waved his hands and his eyes popped, and when he buried his "beautiful Annabel Lee," he looked just like Laura Epps when she's about to cry.

Homer Fink split us up. It was the first time the class had really been laughing with him and not at him.

Miss Pierce laughed so hard she had to dry the tears from her eyes. Before the class voted, she explained that the oratory contest wasn't really meant to be a joke-telling contest but that she saw no reason why a good parody wouldn't make a valid entry.

No one but Homer was sure what "parody" meant. But it didn't make any difference. For the first time in the history of class 9-1, Phillip Moore was our second choice.

2

ALL THE REST OF THAT DAY the kids kept telling Homer he was a riot. In history class when Mr. Bean called on him to explain the feudal system, Homer said, "Humor is a derivative of the Latin word *humor*. Its original meaning was liquid."

The class started laughing, and nothing Mr. Bean said could quiet them. Just the sight of Homer Fink rising to speak was enough to convulse Brian Spitzer, and Trudy Deal bit a hole right through her handkerchief. Homer finally did explain feudalism. He told us the word came from the Latin *feodum or feudum,* a fee. "It is important to understand that the most pressing need of the late Roman and early medieval society was protection against attacks by invading tribes or neighbors," Homer went on. But you could hardly hear him. Mr. Bean finally had to send Brian to the principal's office and threaten Trudy with detention to make the class settle down.

After school Homer walked me home.

"Hail, Richard," he called as I started up the street. Homer bounded in front of me, walking backward and swinging his arms. He almost hit Marvin Bloom in the face with his schoolbag, which wouldn't have been such a good idea because Marvin was big for his age and liked to fight.

"Hi, Homer," I said. "You were great, but what happened to Demosthenes?"

He smiled, dropped his schoolbag, and clapped his hands. It was a warm fall day and most of the boys were wearing jackets or sweaters. Only Homer was wearing an overcoat. His face was flushed and I knew he must be hot, but he didn't seem to mind.

"Got a ball? Let's catch," he said to me. "Throw the sphere. Flip the pellet. Chuck the apple." He cupped his hands and rolled his shoulders and kept moving backward all the time.

I had a rubber ball in my pocket and I threw it to him.

12

"Strike one," called Homer. "You are Carl Owen Hubbell born June 22, 1903, Carthage, Missouri, and you have just succeeded in throwing a third strike past Joseph Edward Cronin, born October 21, 1906, San Francisco, California, for the fifth successive strikeout in the All-Star contest, 1934." Homer never could understand what it was about baseball that got me.

After a long windup he threw the ball back.

"Catchers don't wind up," I advised him. "Just cock your arm and throw."

"Absolutely," said Homer Fink and he held up a target. "Is this preferable? Throw, Richard, lay on your meteor."

Homer's overcoat was dragging and he seemed to have forgotten that he had discarded his schoolbag. He was holding up a target and trying hard to look like a catcher. I knew I'd have to throw fast before he lost his balance.

I let the ball fly and Homer caught it.

"You're getting better," I told him. "We'll make an Oriole out of you yet."

The Baltimore Orioles were our home team and once my dad had taken Homer with us to a game. Homer had wanted to know what to do. "Root," my father told him. It was getting a little embarrassing with Homer screaming to the players, "Blast forth beyond the great horizon. For victory. For honor. And Lord Calvert!" My dad finally occupied Homer with a scorecard

13

and Homer Fink spent the afternoon making up a code for recording the game.

I reminded Homer about his bookbag and we had a one-hand catch the rest of the way to my house. It took us about an hour to get home —which is pretty slow considering I live a little more than a mile from school. An Edsel passed us on the street. I had never seen nor heard of an Edsel until Homer told me all about the history of that automobile. He was also in the mood for stepping on leaves and breathing real deep in and out.

"Nothing compares to breathing on a clear fall afternoon to let you know you are alive," said Homer Fink. I know I'm alive anyway, but that isn't the kind of thing I would say to Homer unless I were ready for a long speech. And I was thinking we might go to the park and toss around a football.

My mother was in the kitchen. She was feeding my twin brothers who are six months old, and Mom is always feeding them when she's not rocking them to sleep or washing diapers. I have another brother, Pete, who is two and a half. He was sitting by the sink and opening and closing the door to the pot compartment. Pete would open the door wide and then slam it shut and scream and laugh as if he had just done something great. Pete can hardly talk. It sounded to me as if he were saying, "Me. Door. Me. Door." The twins were strapped to cradles where they could take their bottles and keep an eye on Pete. They were gurgling and looking at Pete with big open eyes. You just knew they thought he was the greatest.

Homer said, "Greetings, Mrs. Sanders. How fare Romulus and Remus this good day?"

"They're just fine, Homer. Thriving." My mother adjusted the bun at the back of her neck. She really flipped when Homer started talking like a character in Shakespeare. I know Mom would have never come up with two names like Romulus and Remus if Homer hadn't suggested she name them after the founders of Rome. (He had been around when Mom was "in a family way" and it was Homer who first identified my mother as pregnant. " 'Pregnant' has far more possibilities than 'being in a family way.' ")

"And what elixir hath thee prepared for us, enchanting lady?" continued Homer.

"Homer, you're too much," my mother said. And I could tell right off she was so tickled she would have done most anything to live up to Homer's expectations. Maybe even opened a bottle of Coke, which we were only allowed to drink on special occasions because of what it does to your teeth.

But milk with honey is what Homer enjoys

15

most, and that's what we had. Homer drank in great long swallows and there was a big ring about his mouth when he was done.

"Hey, Homer, tide's out," I said. It was a signal to let him know he needed a napkin.

Usually Homer didn't have much to say to the twins. I could never figure out what anybody can say to babies, but Mom claims you have to talk to them or they never learn words. Once when Homer and I were baby-sitting for Pete and the twins and they were giving us a hard time, I followed my mother's advice. I gave them some words all right. "Vulgate, slang, and profanity," was the way Homer identified my vocabulary. He was more interested than my brothers. "What depths of society you have tapped," said Homer Fink. "What incredible idioms you have encountered."

A couple of days later Homer had found a book that gave all the meanings. "You shouldn't address your siblings in such phrases," he advised me. "It diverts the noble aspirations of the spirit." But later he went on to tell me a few words that even I hadn't heard before.

After the milk and honey, Homer and I would be on our way. It was all Pete could do to stand up and say, "Me. Me. Me." But this was the afternoon of the oratory tryouts and Homer seemed willing to try anything.

Homer dropped to his knees and let Pete sit

on his back and started talking to Romy and Remo in Latin. Homer was reciting Caesar's *Gallic War*, but from the way the twins split up and Pete was screaming you'd think he was telling them about the original chicken who crossed the street. It was his expression and the way he moved his hands that got to them mostly. There was Homer with his long red hair and freckled face with his overcoat still on. (He never took it off when visiting because he was sure he would forget it.) He said, *"Omnia,"* and started wiggling his ears and bouncing Pete on his back. Then he was quiet and when everything was still Homer said, *"Gallia."* He went through the same routine. And finally knocked off the whole paragraph to a background of squealing infants and Pete screaming, "Me. Me. Me."

My mother was as surprised as I was. It wasn't until Pete finally fell and started screaming that Homer stopped. My mother picked up Pete and hugged him and put a damp cloth to his forehead. Homer was all shook up. There aren't any babies in his house. He's an only child, and I guess he thought Pete had a brain tumor and wouldn't grow up normally because of him. When Homer is scared he bobs off the balls of his feet, beats his chest, and pulls his hair. I kept telling Homer it was all right. Pete fell at least once an hour and usually all he needed

17

was a little hugging and loving to feel better again. Pete was more scared than hurt.

Mom held Pete up close to Homer to reassure him. "Tell cousin Homer you're all right."

"The brain is such a delicate instrument," said Homer Fink. "The slightest damage to area seventeen can cause impairment of vision."

That's one of Homer's troubles. He knows so much, he has more to worry about than other people.

"Great Zeus—smile upon us," continued Homer. "Grant the child, Peter, the mercy of Olympus." Homer was praying. He knew all that Latin and Greek and he really believed the gods were up there watching us, fighting it out to see who had his way on earth.

"Peter is perfectly all right." My mother touched Homer's shoulder to reassure him and then looked to me. "Tell Homer he didn't hurt Peter. He doesn't believe me."

"Hey, Pete, want a piece of candy?" I showed him a sourball that had been stuck in the bottom of my pants pocket. Pete held his breath. He looked me over for a couple of seconds, trying to decide whether to give a full blast or reach for the sourball. Finally, he turned his head away and started kicking and screaming. I guess he figured I was only teasing.

I gave the sourball to Homer. "Go ahead— you have to bribe the animals," I told him.

18

After rinsing the sourball, Homer brought it to Pete who took it like he was doing Homer a big favor. He stopped crying and sucked in his breath and then threw the sourball across the room and shouted, *"Omni— Omni— Omni—."* He poked his fingers at Homer and started laughing and crying at the same time.

"I think he's trying to say *'omnia,'*" my mother advised Homer Fink. "You seem to have made an impression."

That was all the encouragement Homer needed. He started wiggling his ears and reciting in Latin again while Pete screamed, *"Omni— Omni—."* It wasn't exactly perfect Latin, but I know plenty of kids our age who don't come that close.

The twins were gurgling and smiling their toothless smiles and ignoring the bottles altogether.

It could have gone on like that forever, but then Pete wanted to ride on Homer's back again and my mother decided Pete was grouchy and demanding because it was time for his nap. As she carried him from the room, Pete screamed and pointed at Homer. *"Omni— Omni—"* he said and Homer answered, *"Omnia. Pax vobiscum."*

3

DRUID HILL PARK in Baltimore has tennis courts and a public swimming pool, a zoo, and lots of places for picnics. There are also a boat lake and an aquarium, football fields and baseball diamonds. But the place Homer Fink likes most is the big hill overlooking Jones Falls. It only takes fifteen minutes to get there from my house and we go there a lot. There's not much to do up there on the hill but talk and think and look for the shepherd who has a dozen sheep.

We saw the shepherd that afternoon. He came up the path from the woods carrying a big staff. There was an old dog with him that ambled along with his nose to the ground, sniffing and wagging his tail and barking at the sheep. The sheep looked dirty and gray. They moved slowly as if they were old and tired, and they stayed close together—probably because they were frightened. Homer and I watched them.

"That man is Pan," said Homer. I didn't pay much attention to Homer. I wanted to run after the shepherd and find out where he was going and where he lived and how come he was raising sheep right in the middle of a big city like Baltimore and did the mayor know he was in Druid Hill Park?

"Don't move," Homer told me. "You'll scare him and he'll disappear."

That didn't make much sense. It was strange all right. You don't see a shepherd in the park every day, but the man was real enough and there was no mistaking the shrill bleat of the sheep.

I listened to Homer and stayed. He had picked this place. He liked it because the trees and woods cut off all signs of the city. With the exception of the dome of the mansion house, there was no reminder of the facilities of a public park. We watched as the shepherd led his flock to a small open field. "It is Pan. I know it's Pan," Homer insisted. There was a distant look about his eyes as if he were looking out the window during math class.

"Knock it off," I told him. "That guy's no more Pan than I'm Brooks Robinson."

I thought that reminding Homer about the third baseman of the Orioles might bring him back to earth. But it didn't.

"Pan routed the Persians at Marathon and now he's here," Homer said.

"And Robinson routed the White Sox, Yankees, and Detroit Tigers, but the Orioles still didn't win the pennant," I replied.

Homer was slipping away from me. He seemed to be taking off. "Look, if you're going to act crazy and stuff like that, I'm going to run right down there and find out who he is whether you like it or not."

Homer held a hand out to block me. "I pray thee, do not move."

"And don't start disguising your voice and pretending to be some kind of actor or William Shakespeare."

"Please, Richard—for me—for our friendship."

Homer didn't ask for favors often and this seemed to mean a whole lot more to him than to me.

"O.K.," I said, "I'll mind my own business. If you're going to carry on as if you were walking in your sleep, that's up to you. But when the men in the white uniforms come to take you away, don't say I didn't warn you."

I had a Scout knife and I scratched a big square in the earth and divided it in half. I guess I would have watched the sheep grazing too, but Homer was so serious and distant it gave me the creeps. I decided to play territory for Homer and me. I aimed the knife and it stuck in the ground. "I just shot for you," I announced to Homer. "You're doing great."

I drew the line through my territory and shot again.

It wasn't until after the shepherd took off that Homer spoke again. He was happy and excited. "The son of Hermes is in our midst. We've seen him. You must promise me, Richard, that you won't tell anyone."

I concentrated on the game. "You're down to your last three feet. If I were you I'd start shooting for myself and quick."

Homer took the knife, stepped into what remained of his territory, and fired. The knife landed smack in the middle of my ground.

"Pretty good. If you keep that up I'll start believing that stuff about the gods entering the bodies of men—all that mythology you're so hot on."

"No . . . no," said Homer. "That *was* Pan—in person. Πάν . Didn't you see his goat's legs and ears and horns?"

"You shoot again," I said. "Get your feet on the earth and concentrate on what you're doing."

Homer placed himself within the boundary of his land. His next shot stuck, leaving me a few inches.

"You been practicing in your spare time?" I drew the lines for him. There was no chance of getting Homer to do that. He was too excited.

"Pan was here in Druid Hill Park." Homer looked toward the sky. "Like Socrates I pray to him—great god Pan—for inward beauty."

"Comb your hair and you won't have to pray so much," I said. "You'll never make this last shot."

He didn't.

It was getting toward twilight and we were on our way home when Homer said, "The gods have sent me a sign and I must read it well, Richard. Do I have your word that you will speak of this to no one?"

"You think I'm nuts," I said. "It's rough enough explaining about the shepherd. I'm not about to try to convince anybody he's a goat-man."

"I knew I could trust you," said Homer Fink. "Neither God nor man hath a better companion for life's adventures. When I read the signs— you shall be the first to know."

4

"THE SIGNS," as Homer called them, continued to appear until the morning of the oratory contest. Following the class tryouts Homer didn't talk about the finals. He was on a Plato kick. I wouldn't have known if I hadn't been curious about some doodling on his homework notebook. I saw: συνειδὼς ἐμαυτῷ ἀμαθίαν.

We were sitting in the library when I asked Homer what that meant.

"I am conscious of my own ignorance," said Homer Fink. I suppose that should have given me something to think about, but it didn't.

I had finished my homework and was rolling up scrap paper to shoot into the wastebasket.

Mrs. Creel, the assistant librarian, was the study-hall proctor. She had this way of sitting with a book in front of her and her hands cupped on her forehead. Her eyes were covered so that we couldn't see if she was sleeping. Mrs. Creel had gray hair and she wore long dresses that came down almost to her ankles. Some of the faculty people called her Dr. Creel. There was a rumor that Mrs. Creel had the highest academic degree in the school. But her family had been killed in an automobile accident a long time ago and she wasn't interested in teaching or doing anything else but working in the library filing books and supervising the study period. I was sure she was asleep.

I fired a paper clip into the wastebasket. Mrs. Creel did not react to the metallic ring. And when I shot a ball of paper toward the basket she didn't raise her head.

Brian Spitzer signaled from the other side of the room that he was going to try a shot. He missed. Cindy Walsh tried a hook from the fifth seat in the third row and it swished in.

Soon, most of the class was rolling up paper balls and throwing them at the basket. Phillip Moore and Homer Fink were the only students who didn't join the game. Phillip was reading a book of American history as if his life depended on it. And Homer was writing notes: "I am convinced there is no hope for cities unless philosophers became rulers or rulers philosophers."

I didn't pay much attention to Homer. By

this time my idea of throwing paper balls at the basket was really catching on. From all over the room paper went flying toward Mrs. Creel's open basket.

I just sat quietly watching all those paper balls fly through the air. I didn't want to feel conceited, but I couldn't help being proud. I understood how Thomas Alva Edison must have felt when the lights started going on or Alexander Graham Bell when the phones began ringing. The only trouble was that everybody threw at once and the paper balls collided, falling short of the mark. It was Brian Spitzer's suggestion to divide the room into two teams. The right side could shoot against the left. We arranged a firing order, shooting one at a time.

The floor was loaded with paper balls. Trudy Deal's shot landed on the eraser ledge in front of the blackboard and Danny Bachman's layup was on top of Mrs. Creel's inkwell.

It was Homer's turn. I would have skipped him, but our team was a point behind and we needed every chance.

I nudged Homer with my elbow and handed him a sheet of loose-leaf paper. "At the basket. Shoot," I whispered.

Homer said, "For a chaplet of wild olive." He popped up from his seat and let the paper ball fly. It hit the blackboard and bounced off just as Mr. Muncrief, the assistant principal, entered. Homer's paper ball caught him on the right sleeve.

"What is the meaning of this?" Mr. Muncrief demanded. You could have a riot in the schoolyard or a fire in the boy's lavatory and Mr. Muncrief's first words would be, "What is the meaning of this?" We all sat up straight and folded our hands on our desks. But not Homer.

"The chaplet of olives," Homer continued, "was the prize awarded to the winners of the Olympic games. The games, traditionally held once every four years, were founded in 776 B.C."

"That will be enough." Mr. Muncrief rubbed his sleeve to remind Homer that he had been struck by the paper ball.

"Yes, sir." Homer Fink stood there smiling and looking off into the distance as if he had never heard of an assistant principal before and didn't have a thought about detention.

Mr. Muncrief continued across the room, kicking at the paper balls as if they were land mines. "What is the meaning of this?" he asked again.

"According to Plato's discourse in the *Laws*, extremes are bad," said Homer Fink. "Too much freedom or too much despotism is equally dangerous. What we must have is a mixed constitution."

"I would say this is extreme indeed," said Mr.

Muncrief. "And let me assure you I shall get to the bottom of it. I will know the reason why."

"Begging your pardon, sir," Homer said, "I doubt very much if you will arrive at a dialectic to establish the reason why."

Mr. Muncrief thumped his fingers on a desk in the first row. "You may be seated, Fink."

Homer said, "Thank you, sir." Homer was always saying "thank you" and "excuse me." He was just about the only boy alive who could say "thank you" and really mean it and get somebody hysterically angry at him.

Mr. Muncrief said, "I'll have more to say to you later—young man." There was no doubt in my mind that Homer wouldn't be going up to the hill that afternoon. I was sure he was in for a long session of staying in after school. "And now, with Dr. Creel's kind permission—continue with your research, Doctor—we'll make short work of this." Mr. Muncrief glanced at Mrs. Creel, who was still asleep. Then he looked across the room, staring into the eyes of each and every one of us. I guess he thought that would give us a guilty conscience and everybody would own up. "Who did it?" he said. "Who threw the paper around the room? Who cares so little for his classroom that he turns it into a pigpen? Who?"

Homer Fink was back on his feet.

"Yes, Homer, what is it now?"

Homer stood with his arms at his side and his chin tilted upward. He looked like a soldier facing a firing squad or, as he would say, a slave on his way to wrestle with the lions at the Colosseum. "I confess," said Homer Fink.

Mr. Muncrief let out a long sigh. For a moment he seemed about to let Homer have it, but then Mr. Muncrief started to stare at Homer's tie which had flapped over his jacket button. The bottom part was much longer than the top. Mr. Muncrief seemed to forget all about the paper balls and the room looking like a pigpen. He started from the front of the class and headed right for Homer. Mr. Muncrief's eyes never left Homer's tie.

In less than a minute Mr. Muncrief had retied Homer Fink's wool plaid. It was probably the first time since Homer had first put it on that the bottom points touched. That seemed to make Mr. Muncrief feel a lot better.

"Very well, Homer, thank you for being so honest," said the assistant principal. "I'm not going to threaten you boys and girls. No, indeed I'm not. I came to make an announcement and I'm going to do exactly that. When I've left—and I expect no procrastinating—I will expect each and every one of you who was involved in this destructive play to clean up."

Mr. Muncrief was back at the front of the room, thumping his fingers on a desk. "As you all know, this Friday at general assembly we will be having our twenty-fifth annual oratory and declamation contest. I understand that this class has selected two very fine, outstanding young orators." Mr. Muncrief's right hand moved to his jacket pocket. He pulled out a white card. "Yes, indeed, class 9-1 will be represented by—Phillip Moore. Phillip, will you please stand up and—?" Mr. Muncrief stopped speaking and examined the card. It couldn't have been more than two seconds, but the class started to snicker. Just the thought of Homer and the oratory contest was enough to shake up Trudy Deal.

"Well, now—I see you will be joining us, Homer." Mr. Muncrief tried to sound as if Homer Fink as a contestant in the oratory contest was the most natural thing in the world.

Brian Spitzer started to laugh.

"And what is the meaning of this?" Mr. Muncrief demanded of Brian.

"My speech is a parody," Homer replied. "That's why Brian is laughing, Mr. Muncrief. That's the meaning."

"Yes—well—thank you, Homer. And I shall be looking forward to hearing it."

Mr. Muncrief was just going to have to learn to stop asking for the meaning of things with Homer Fink in the room.

"And, boys and girls, if I may have your attention, I should like to talk to you for just a moment about the implications of a contest such as this. Let me ask you—what do you think is the purpose of oratory?"

Phillip Moore had his hand up first. "It's a way of entertaining and informing."

"Very good, indeed," said Mr. Muncrief. "Anything else?"

Neil Machen said it was a way to give sermons.

Alma Melchere raised her hand and pressed out of her seat as if she had to deliver a message from the President of the United States. When Mr. Muncrief called on her she said, "Oratory is making speeches."

Then Jerry Trout told us oratory was good on Decoration Day and the Fourth of July to make us patriotic. Bernice Macht said, "When the people on television talk about things and sell toothpaste and cars—that's a kind of oratory."

There were still a couple of hands raised when Mr. Muncrief signaled that we had enough class participation. "Let's try another approach. Now someone mentioned—I believe it was Phillip—that oratory is a way of informing and one young lady suggested that oratory is also a means of selling. Can you think of a kind of oratory that we are all exposed to at one particular season of the year—a kind of speech-making that is very important to all of us?"

Alma Melchere looked as if she were thinking hard enough to burst, and Neil Machen kept half-raising his hand—trying to let us know he was close to the answer but not quite sure. But no one volunteered.

"Suppose you try that one, Homer," said Mr. Muncrief. It was obvious he didn't have much experience with our class. Homer Fink was staring out the window again. A few strands of long red hair had fallen across his forehead. It seemed to me it was right in his eye but Homer didn't notice. He was just staring out that window and you would have needed a telescope to locate his thoughts.

"Homer . . . Homer Fink . . . I'm speaking to you," said the assistant principal. Mr. Muncrief didn't seem the least bit irritated. I think tying Homer's tie made him feel as if they were pals. "Homer, this is Mr. Muncrief speaking," he went on slowly. "I've asked a question—"

There was no answer from Homer Fink.

Mr. Muncrief looked very disappointed.

Quietly the first chorus began: "Fink. Fink. Fink."

We had to bring Homer back—to get him with it. "Fink. Fink. Fink."

"Homer, I'm asking a question . . . I expect a reply. What is the meaning of this?"

Homer's head jolted forward. His eyes

blinked. "The whole virtue of the philosopher-king is dependent upon a personal knowledge of good," said Homer.

I had a feeling he was still working out Plato. But most of the class found Homer's answer a riot. Mr. Muncrief allowed several seconds of laughter before raising his hand for silence. "The question was: What is a major use of oratory? Homer, perhaps you could tell us." Mr. Muncrief was still being Homer's friend.

Homer began by discussing the rules of rhetoric, but it wasn't long before he got around to mentioning how important speech-making was to win the hearts and minds of people. Mr. Muncrief interrupted a few times with some questions. At last Homer Fink said we all heard a lot of speech-making before Election Day, because it was one of the ways candidates got themselves elected to office. That was exactly what Mr. Muncrief wanted to hear. He had come to our class to tell us that within the next few weeks the pupils of our school were going to elect a student government. "Two students will be elected to represent each class and one boy or girl will have the honor and challenge of being the president of our student council. How do you like that?"

Alma Melchere started clapping her hands and screwing her face up. She was so excited you would have thought the Supreme Court had declared homework unconstitutional. Trudy Deal sighed and looked as if she were going to cry. Neil Machen asked Brian Spitzer to nominate him.

Mr. Muncrief signaled for quiet and then he went on to tell us about the responsibilities of the citizens in a democracy. He told us to be especially watchful for the good leaders, and he hinted that the oratory contest might be an opportunity to discover a candidate.

Mr. Muncrief reminded us he had a number of other classes to visit and that "time is short." Again he addressed himself to Mrs. Creel. Her hand remained cupped over her eyes. All we could see was a happy satisfied grin about her lips. Her head bobbed forward and back as if to say, "Yes . . . I approve."

"Thank you for letting me intrude," Mr. Muncrief told the study-hall proctor. "You are perfectly right to proceed with your research, and now if I may I'll just ask young Fink to see to it that the papers are cleaned up and I'll be off." With that, Mr. Muncrief went to the door. "Homer," he called across the room, "let's see you take charge and get the job done."

Homer was busily scribbling in his notebook.

"Homer—Homer," Mr. Muncrief called again. "This is Mr. Muncrief, Homer." Mr. Muncrief seemed to believe that Homer couldn't identify his voice and that that was the difficulty with their communication. It took another chorus of "Fink, Fink, Fink," before Homer finally got the point.

The door had closed behind Mr. Muncrief and Homer moved to the front of the room when Mrs. Creel dropped her hand from her forehead. Her head dropped forward and then opening her eyes wide she slapped her hand on the desk. "Let's have no more of that!"

It wasn't easy to know what she meant. The fact was that most of us were sitting quietly with our hands folded on our desks. We hadn't completely recovered from having Mr. Muncrief in the room.

"I said 'no more,'" Mrs. Creel went on. "Study hall is a time for attending to our assignments, reading, and thought. Silence is the rule. You there—" Mrs. Creel nodded in the direction of Homer Fink. "Young man—take your seat immediately. I do not recall having given you permission to come to the front."

Alma Melchere said, "Mr. Muncrief—Mr. Muncrief told Homer to take charge and . . ."

Mrs. Creel interrupted Alma Melchere. "Perhaps I am mistaken, but I have no impression that you raised your hand to be recognized."

"No, ma'am," said Alma and she raised her hand and sat up so stiff she looked like a statue of the Bird Woman who led Lewis and Clark across the Rockies.

"Did I not make myself clear?" Mrs. Creel continued to Homer. "Did I not say to take your seat?"

Homer started back to his place.

"And this will go on report, Mr. Fink. You have not gotten away with this little caper."

Brian Spitzer raised his hand. It was pretty clear to everybody in the class that Mrs. Creel had slept through Mr. Muncrief's visit. And now Homer was going to have to stay after school or bring in a note from home because of the teacher's mistake. "Yes, Brian," said Mrs. Creel.

Brian Spitzer stood up and tried to hold back a laugh. In a way it was ridiculous, but Mrs. Creel was old and there had been that accident. I felt sorry for her.

"Mr. Muncrief was in the room," Brian sputtered. "We all saw him. He told Homer to—"

"That will be enough," said Mrs. Creel. "You may sit down, young man. The rest of you may return to your studies."

There was the sound of conversation in the room. "Quiet, please. May I remind you this is a study hall?" Mrs. Creel's voice didn't sound so confident.

"Mr. Muncrief was here and you slept through," Neil Machen called from the middle of the room. "You can't punish Homer for that."

Neil had spoken out of turn, but the class agreed with him. This was the first time I could remember seeing a teacher so obviously in the wrong, and most of the class was excited by it.

Someone said, "Yes, you were asleep."

And we heard, "We can prove it."

"Mr. Muncrief is a witness."

Mrs. Creel's head moved from one side of the room to the other. Each comment seemed to be a slap. I could see she really wasn't as tough as she pretended. I guess when you get to the point where you fall asleep in class, you know it. And Mrs. Creel didn't need our class to make her feel bad.

I don't know how it was that Homer Fink managed to make his voice heard above all the others. And I certainly don't understand what it was about Homer that made us all quiet down to listen to him. But there was Homer standing at his seat, scratching his chin, and trying hard to get to the bottom of something. "In history class this afternoon," said Homer, "we learned that there is a difference between the meaning of 'constitution' in the United States and Great Britain. I'm not so sure I understand that. Do you think you could explain, Dr. Creel?"

The Constitution didn't have anything to do with our problem, but the mention of it and having Homer Fink bring it up made everybody quiet down.

Mrs. Creel adjusted her glasses. She was

study-hall proctor and we were supposed to ask her questions, but I've been at P.S. 79 for three years and I never heard any student ask Mrs. Creel anything more serious than, "Could I be excused to get drink of water?"

"Indeed, Homer, the use of the word 'constitution' in its plural sense made one of its rare appearances in English history in those Constitutions of Clarendon, 1164." Mrs. Creel's face brightened and I remembered having heard that she was once a history teacher at a girls' college. The next thing we knew she was up at the blackboard writing words like "Magna Charta," and making lists to show the difference.

"Although in the United States—because our law is written—an act can be unconstitutional and therefore illegal, in England the usage 'unconstitutional' would mean 'unconventional.' Let's try it this way. It is illegal for you not to go to school because that is part of our law. But it is unconventional not to raise your hand in class or to throw paper balls at the wastebasket. It is unconventional because it is usually not done."

Nobody except Phillip Moore, who wanted to be a lawyer, was excited about that constitutional stuff. But when the bell rang for the end of study hall, Dr. Creel had us all convinced she knew a lot about the Constitution—which was something considering her long silence.

On the way home from school that afternoon I told Homer Fink, "You sure did get Creel off the hook."

"The Magna Charta did that," said Homer. "It is as the wise men say—'knowledge is power.'"

"Knowledge, my elbow. If you hadn't known that Creel was a history teacher and had all that information on constitutional systems there would have been a revolution."

Homer shrugged and said, "Did you know that when the maximum width of a skull is less than seventy-five per cent of the maximum length, the skull is called 'dolichocephalic'—or long-headed?"

I said, "No, but Mickey Mantle batted .300 in 1952, his first full season with the New York Yankees."

".311," Homer corrected me. "Mickey Charles Mantle, born October 20, 1931, Spavinaw, Oklahoma."

"Ah, come off it, Homer," I said. "You're trying to skip the subject. But you gave Creel a chance to bail out this morning. And I was wondering why."

"We dreamers have to stick together," said Homer Fink. And with that he started backward across the street.

5

I CALLED FOR HOMER the morning of the oratory contest. We have to be in our seats at eight forty-five and it takes fifteen minutes to get from Homer's house to P.S. 79. I arrived at the Finks' house on Park Avenue at eight o'clock. Park Avenue in Baltimore is not the same as the Park Avenue in New York. You wouldn't find the richest people in town living there. Mostly, the houses have been in the same family for a long time. They are three- and four-story brownstones or gray brick. Some have attics. I guess lots of people move from Park Avenue because they get tired of walking all the steps or because, as they say, "the neighborhood is changing."

Mrs. Fink opened the door. "Good morning, Richard. My, what a lovely day you've brought us."

I said, "Hi, Mrs. Fink. Is Homer up yet?"

"I do believe he is," said Mrs. Fink.

"If you don't mind, I'll run up to his room and get him," I said.

"What a perfectly splendid idea," said Homer's mother.

"I am sure Homer will be delighted to see you."

Homer's family is different from mine. There is just Homer and his father, who teaches Greek and Latin at the University, and Mrs. Fink, who is usually singing or playing the lute. Everybody is always very busy in the Fink house. I don't think I've ever seen Mr. Fink when there wasn't a book in his lap or stuck in his pocket or open and resting on a table because he'd just put it down so I wouldn't think I'd interrupted him. Mrs. Fink is usually smiling and she can think of more nice things to say to me than anybody I've ever known. Take a thing like opening the door. All I have to do is knock and Mrs. Fink greets me as if I personally were responsible for letting in the outside world. Even when it's raining she'll say things like, "A little rain at last. I'm sure the farmers will be grateful to you." Or, "Rain! How wonderful, Richard. You've remembered the azaleas."

Anyway, I started up the steps to Homer's room—which was no easy trip. There was a bedspread covering the first four steps and one of Homer's slippers on the first landing. Argus, the Finks' dog, was springing at my heels as I moved. I like pets, but it took me a long time to warm up to Argus. Homer tells me Argus is a Maltese and has a great history. "Neither you nor I have an ancestry as distinguished as Argus, Richard. It will do us both well to remember our place."

Argus has a sharp nose and bushy tail and I guess he knows he can get away with murder with the Finks. But it doesn't work with me. We used to have a beagle and the one thing I know about pets is that you have to let them know exactly what you expect of them. I took a swat at Argus' tail. "Don't you nip at me," I told him, "ancestry or no ancestry."

Argus may have had a lineage, but he wasn't much on courage. He retreated, barking to have the last word.

There was music coming from Homer Fink's room and the alarm was ringing. As usual, the floor was covered with books and clothes and papers.

Homer was sound asleep with a pillow over his head.

"Hey, are you trying to commit suicide?" I pulled the pillow away from him and slapped it against his face. "It's ten minutes after eight, Demosthenes—the Spartans are at the city gates."

"The oratory contest!" exclaimed Homer Fink. He bounded out of bed, picked up the first pair of trousers he saw, and started to pull them over his pajama pants.

"Homer, are you planning to take a nap in school today?"

Homer didn't get the point. "I must win this contest, Richard," he said. "The signs are becoming clear." He searched around the floor and found a shirt. He put it on over the pajama top.

"You're wearing your pajamas to school, Homer," I told him.

Homer Fink shrugged. "It's Friday. We don't have gym."

It took me a couple of seconds to figure that out. I decided what Homer meant was that there was no chance of discovery.

"What do the signs add up to?" I asked. "Are you going to start grazing cattle in Droodle Park?"

Homer winced. "If I were mayor of Baltimore I would fine every citizen who says Droodle for Druid Hill." Homer hopped on top of his bed. His shirttail was out and he was barefoot. "But I am not ready to be mayor. I am going to run for president. The gods have called upon me to lead my people."

Homer had made announcements like that before. Once he had me convinced that all the United Nations needed was a visit from Homer Fink. We were going up to New York and talk things over with the Russians and Americans. The way I remember it, Homer wanted a statue of Zeus in the Security Council or something like that.

Homer jumped from the bed pulling the covers with him. "This is my opportunity. I'll have a captive audience. I'm going to explicate my philosophy in front of the entire student body. I may be crowned by acclamation."

I was going to remind Homer about the difference between electing the president of the school and crowning a king, but there was a bulge in the center of his mattress and I wanted to find out what it was.

"All the signs portend a victory." Homer pulled a blue sock onto his right foot and a brown onto the left. "My triumph in the class contest was the first success I've had in competition. The shepherd in the park—my liaison with the school administration. I've been called. I have definitely been called, Richard." Homer bounded across the room and picked a tie from a group that had collected at one end of a hanger. It was blue with a gold palm tree. It must have been three inches wide and I don't remember ever seeing another tie shaped like it.

"What's under your mattress?" I asked.

"And you, Richard, will be my Talleyrand—my Boswell—my Tonto."

"If you're not going to tell me, I'll look."

"You will be my Mark Hanna, my James Farley—my very own Bobby Kennedy."

I lifted up the mattress and found a new baseball glove. "What's this doing here, Homer? A baseball glove under the mattress? I don't get it."

"I need you, Richard." Homer forced his feet into his shoes without untying the laces. He thrust his hand toward me. "Give me your pledge."

"You know you're ruining a good fielder's glove."

"Nonsense. There are seasons and cycles. That is the order of our universe. Of what use is a baseball glove in the fall? It must rest and hibernate to cultivate its pocket." Homer took the glove and bounced a fist into the pocket. Then he returned it to the mattress. "Next spring—you'll be proud of me, Richard. I'm going to play John Evers to your Joe Tinkers —short to second, poetry in motion."

Homer ate two figs, a date, and a banana for breakfast. Mrs. Fink handed him a paper bag with his lunch and kissed him on the forehead. The Professor came from the breakfast table, brushing ashes from his tweed vest, looking over the rimless glasses that seemed about to fall from his nose. He mumbled something in Latin, clasped Homer's forearm and wished him well.

We made it up Park Avenue in eight minutes flat.

Homer Fink couldn't wait to get to school. He didn't daydream once during the first two classes, and when the students gathered in the auditorium Homer Fink was the only contestant who seemed really happy to be in the oratory contest.

6

Mr. MUNCRIEF had the first two rows of the auditorium reserved for the orators. They stood by their places, trying to look brave. The boys were fastening and unfastening their jacket buttons, hitching up their pants, and looking over their notes. The girls, dressed in their best, checked their make-up.

Only Homer Fink was looking around the auditorium. He was waving to our class and holding up two fingers signaling "O" for onward. When we sang "America," Homer's voice could be heard as far back as the tenth row and he pledged allegiance to the flag so loudly you would have thought an un-American activities committee was taking notes.

After the opening ceremonies, Mr. Muncrief said a "few words" that went on for fifteen minutes and then Miss Sadie P. Everswell, the principal, spoke. Miss Everswell tried to make the contestants "comfortable."

Each contestant had five minutes for a recitation. No one was supposed to talk longer than that. Mrs. Newthal, the math teacher, was the official timer. The secretary of the senior class, Irma Micklisch, had the job of standing at four minutes and raising her hand when the speaker's time was up.

Miss Everswell introduced the first speaker.

A boy from 7-5, who must have skipped four times or else he was the smallest kid for his age in the world, came bouncing up to the stage. He started talking when he was two steps from the microphone.

"It looked extremely rocky for the Mudville nine that day," the seventh-grader began. He wasn't using the microphone and I could just about make out what he was saying from my seat in the center of the auditorium.

Mr. Muncrief rushed back to center stage, directed the timekeeper to stop the clock and adjusted the microphone. He had to let it all the way down to the base and the seventh-grader had to stand on tiptoes.

"The score stood two to four with but one inning left to play," the seventh-grader continued from where he had left off. He wasn't saying one more word than he had to. It's easy enough to perform in your homeroom with only your teacher and friends in the audience, but most kids choke up in the auditorium.

I wasn't paying much attention to the speakers. They were running through Kipling's poems and Longfellow, and a couple took shots at the preamble to the Constitution. Elaine Steigmar made a speech about one world. Elaine has long, black hair and big eyes and there's no doubt about the fact that she matured early. Brian Spitzer was sitting right on the edge of his chair all through Elaine's talk and I could hear Brian whispering, "You said it, Elaine. Tell them again." That was really something, considering that Brian is never interested in history or current events.

Patty Esposito told us about the death of her dog. I guess she wanted us to cry. When Patty's talk was over she got a great hand. Some of the girls in her class even stood up and it wasn't just because she was the class president. Patty had a sad expression about her face. It seemed winning the contest wasn't important to her. Patty wanted us to think all she cared about was that her "beloved Spot" had been run over by a truck. I happen to know Patty's brother Tony. Tony is a great guy for a catch or to go with to the Hippodrome for Saturday movies and a stage show. But usually Tony is busy because he has six sisters and has to do all the chores like taking out the garbage and raking the yard and walking the dog. I didn't clap much for Patty.

Little Louie Bannerman got almost as great an ovation as Patty. Little Louie is skinny and wears glasses. He's on the honor roll all the time and with the exception of Homer Fink, Louie is the best student at 79. (Once Homer led the honor roll with an average of 99, but more often he loses out because he only does his homework in his head or writes wild answers to essay questions. For example, Homer almost failed eighth-grade history when he answered a question on the causes of the Civil War with an essay on the origin of the Peloponnesian War.) Louie's father is a doctor and that's what Louie wants to be. He recited the Hippocratic oath, and I was one of the people who clapped real hard for Louie.

Our class spoke last and Phillip Moore was on before Homer. Phillip has a clear voice with a slight Southern accent. He was born in Mississippi, but that Southern accent goes over as if he came from the Eastern Shore. It really wows the teachers. They are always calling Phillip a "real Southern gentleman," which he is—but not because he comes from the Eastern Shore of Maryland and lives on a plantation or anything like that. Phillip's father works for an insurance company and he got transferred from Biloxi to Baltimore.

Phillip recited parts of John F. Kennedy's inaugural address. He finished right on the button—just as Irma Micklisch raised her hand. The applause was so terrific you would have thought Phillip was going to plop a stovepipe hat on his head, get in his limousine, and drive right on up to Pennsylvania Avenue.

It seemed to me Homer was really going to have to go some to win first prize. I wasn't feeling too sure about Homer's jokes going over. None of the speakers had even tried to get a laugh and the way everyone was fidgeting in his seat and whispering you could tell it had been a long assembly and the students were restless.

But Homer Fink didn't seem discouraged.

Mr. Muncrief introduced him and waited for a moment until Homer joined him. There was a big smile on Mr. Muncrief's face and he winked to Homer as he adjusted the microphone. I might have felt more confidence if Homer's pajama pants weren't showing beneath the cuffs of his trousers. And, even though I'm not exactly clothes-conscious, it did seem to me that the yellow palm-tree tie was out of place with a plaid shirt.

Homer reached out his hand to greet Mr.

Muncrief. I don't know why he did that. None of the other speakers had thought of doing it. As Homer stretched out his hand, the pajama top was visible beneath his cuffs. But that wasn't what caught Mr. Muncrief's eye. It was all the assistant principal could do to resist re-tying Homer's palm tree. The bottom flap was much longer than the top.

Homer waited until Mr. Muncrief left the stage. Then he started across the platform after him. Homer was headed in the direction of Miss Sadie P. Everswell. I guess he thought it was important to pay his respects to the principal. It must have had something to do with the decorum of the court or protocol or something like that. I'm sure that's the way Homer would have explained it. Miss Everswell acknowledged Homer's greeting with a bow. She looked surprised but pleased. Something happened on Homer's way back to the center of the stage. He only had to walk about twelve feet, but Homer Fink can make a trip like that as dangerous as a journey up the Congo. There was a wire somewhere and Homer found it. His feet did. And for a moment it seemed Homer was doing the twist or offering the first soft-shoe act on the morning's program. When at last he was untangled, there was a ripple of laughter through the auditorium and some applause from the seventh grade.

Homer Fink stood in front of the microphone. He paused and waited for silence. It was very smooth and I was beginning to think that Homer knew what he was doing after all. It could be he read a book on public speaking or studied the advice of his favorite Greek and Roman orators. "Go get them, Homer," I said to myself. "Get this one for the Gip—or Pericles or anybody you like, but talk and talk soon."

"The time has come. The hour is upon us," Homer began. "Arise, my fellow students, and be heard."

The trouble was I could hardly hear Homer Fink's voice, and I'm sure the people in the back of the auditorium and those sitting in the balcony heard nothing at all.

The loud-speaker was off. Homer had disconnected it. Mr. Muncrief started back to the stage, but Homer motioned for him to be seated.

Homer Fink had a speech to make. He had thought it out carefully, preparing his argument. It was complete with gestures and grimaces.

It was deep all right. I'm sure very few of the students would have understood, but all would have been impressed. It's not every day that a boy stands up at a general assembly and tells the teachers how to run the school. But the only impression most of us had was of Homer

Fink moving his mouth silently, flailing his arms and beating his chest, and raising his arms skyward with an occasional plea to Zeus.

Everyone had heard Homer was going to give a funny speech and that's what we were waiting for. After a morning of "The Wreck of the Hesperus" and "Hanging Danny Deever," we needed a few laughs. The only trouble was Homer wasn't trying to be funny. Homer Fink had a message and when Homer felt something, he felt it strongly. As his words failed, Homer's expressions and gestures became more and more passionate.

Finally, Homer bounded across the stage. He was pointing at the audience. "Care! Become involved! Live!" I heard him plead. There were snickers from the seventh grade and laughter from the eighth-grade section.

Homer pulled his tie loose and opened his collar. His pajama top was clearly visible now. It had red candy stripes. (A present from Homer's cousins in Silver Spring who had no children of their own and were always giving Homer gifts.)

"Look at Fink's costume," a girl in the eighth-grade section shrieked.

By this time the ninth grade was finding the performance hilarious. Everybody was laughing. The teachers had given up trying to control their classes. Homer was bringing the school down. Only, it wasn't exactly the way he intended to rip it apart. The response had nothing to do with Homer's deep thought or the passion of his feelings.

"Fink's a riot. He's a screaming idiot," I heard Brian Spitzer say. And if he wasn't sitting two rows behind me I would have punched Brian right in his fat face. I sank deep in my seat. My feet pressed so hard against the auditorium floor I expected to fall to the floor below and land in the gym. It was awful.

Homer Fink went on and on, carried away by the strength of his arguments and the sound of his own voice. But nobody heard another word. The entire school was absorbed by the way Homer dressed and performed.

He walked across the stage with his hands folded behind his back, bouncing off the balls of his feet and thinking deep, and then came to a halt and lined up his fingers. His head was nodding and his eyes were bright and his lips moved, but Irma Micklisch had been on her feet for some time and both her arms were raised and Mrs. Newthal was ringing a bell and no one heard a word.

I suppose Homer Fink would have tried forever if the class bell hadn't sounded. That stopped him long enough for Mr. Muncrief to rush back to the stage, applaud, and put his arm around Homer's shoulder. It took the assistant principal five minutes to quiet down the school and that was really something because it's about all you can do to breathe when Mr. Muncrief signals for silence.

The assistant principal said a few words about laughter being the wine of life or something like that. I guess he had heard enough of Homer's speech to feel inspired because one thing for sure nobody in P.S. 79 drinks wine.

We were on our way back to class when Phillip Moore said, "You were great, Homer. I never laughed so hard. I would have given you first prize."

"You deserved to win," said Homer Fink. "My compliments." And then he said loud enough for everyone to hear, "Of course I broke the rules. I didn't give a speech. I wanted to try a little pantomime."

Homer smiled, but I could see he didn't mean it.

It was the first time I had ever heard Homer Fink make an excuse or seen a sign that he cared what people thought of him.

7

"MACHIAVELLI DREW his conclusions from the nature of mankind ascribing all things to natural causes and fortune. He returned to an approach that had been neglected since the days of Aristotle." Homer Fink thumped me on the back.

"Mr. Bowen called on you twice in general science," I told Homer. "Didn't you hear him say that Machiavelli had nothing to do with paramecium?"

"Of course politics is not an absolute science."

It was three o'clock. School was out for the day. I had expected Homer would be feeling bad about his defeat in the oratory contest.

But after a few minutes of Machiavelli and politics, it was obvious Homer was feeling more like his old self than ever before. He stopped on the corner of Mt. Royal, dropped his books, and looked up at the clock tower of the Baltimore and Ohio Railroad terminal. "Tomorrow afternoon at precisely four o'clock, at the Mt. Royal station, I will cross the Rubicon, Richard."

He said this so loudly that a group of eighth-graders heard him. They came closer to see what Homer Fink was up to. They were laughing before Homer said another word.

"Come on, Homer. Let's go home." I picked up his bookbag and made him take it.

Homer tried again. "The Rubicon is a small stream which formed the boundary between Italy and Gaul. When Caesar crossed it in 49 B.C., it meant a declaration of war against Pompey." I was walking fast and Homer had to run to keep up with me. "Didn't you know that, Richard? What I was trying to say is that I plan to announce my candidacy for the presidency of the student council. 'Crossing the Rubicon' means taking a step which definitely commits a person to a given course of action. I certainly didn't mean to imply I was traveling across the stream by means of the B. and O. Railroad."

"So long, Homer," I said. "I'm not in the

mood for crossing the Rubicon today. I'm going on home and take Pete out for a ride."

Homer Fink took long steps with his back slightly bent and his face down, studying the pattern of the sidewalk. He was wearing his big overcoat and the side pockets bulged. We walked silently a while and then Homer took two halves of a pomegranate from his pocket. He gave one half to me.

We followed the island of green that runs down the middle of Park Avenue. I was balancing my books under my arm and picking the red seeds from the crimson pulp while Homer searched the ground for fall leaves.

He found an oak leaf and put the stem in the lapel of his coat. "I'm going to run for president of the school, Richard. I'd like you to be my campaign manager."

I didn't answer. That made me think about the oratory contest again and the failure of Homer's speech.

He must have read my mind. "I know my talk this morning was a disaster. It didn't work out as I had planned. The craft of politics is subtle and sometimes there are great lessons to learn from small failures."

"You weren't trying to do a pantomime act or anything like that," I told him. "And right now I doubt if anybody in the school will ever take you seriously."

Homer grasped the trunk of a tree and swung himself around. "I'll have to make some adjustments in my public personality. It requires concentrated planning, imagination, and discipline."

I said, "Why don't you join the debating team and try to be captain of that?"

Homer came closer, walking backward in front of me so that I could see his face. "The presidency of the school is the best platform for my ideas."

"Write a letter to the editor of the *Sun*," I suggested. "Or maybe you could do a story for *Scholastic* magazine."

"After we have the student body behind us, we'll be in a position to consolidate the other junior highs of the city," said Homer. "Then, they will come to us."

Homer must have known that I wasn't impressed, because he said, "Imagine we are Athens—one city-state among the many in Greece. In order to spread our influence and realize our ideas, the first thing we have to do is establish a base. Ergo—we begin by unifying Greece."

"Homer, have you taken a good look at P.S. 79 recently? A really good look?"

Homer turned around and walked beside me. He was thinking that over. "The athletic failure of our school is not what concerns me, Richard."

"I was going to say P.S. 79 doesn't have the slightest resemblance to the Acropolis—at least it doesn't to me. And I'm sure most of the students don't know what the Acropolis is and not many more would have the slightest idea what you're talking about when you start that stuff about the Greek city-states."

Homer picked a seed from his pomegranate. "You think I should refrain from classical reference." He popped the seed into his mouth and then nodding said, "I'll consider some restraint during the early stages of the campaign."

I said, "Look, Homer, let's forget it. The plain truth is you wouldn't have any more chance than Trudy Deal to be elected president of the school."

"And that's all the more reason why we must have absolutely expert assistance," said Homer Fink.

My mother was in the kitchen feeding the twins when Homer and I arrived. Pete was in his playpen surrounded by assorted shoes.

"You shouldn't let Pete play with my ski boots," I told my mother.

Mother said, "Good afternoon, Homer. How are you today?"

Pete dropped the ski boot on the other side of the playpen, pointed to Homer, and screamed, *"Omni— Omni—."*

Homer Fink said to my mother, "Greetings to thee, my phantom of delight."

"Why Homer, no man has quoted Wordsworth to me since Mr. Sanders courted me at college." Mother removed a jar of strained applesauce from the warming pan and lifted the top.

"A lovely apparition, sent to be a moment's ornament." Homer took the jar of strained applesauce from my mother's hand. He rinsed the baby spoon and plunked down on the floor in front of the twins.

"Homer Fink, you are absolutely gallant," said my mother. "Not too much applesauce now —a little at a time."

I said, "I was thinking about taking Pete out for a walk, Ma." My voice didn't exactly sound enthusiastic. Homer Fink was becoming more of a politician every moment.

"That's a perfectly splendid idea, darling." My mother lifted Pete from the playpen. "I'll have him in his snowsuit in a jiffy."

Pete called, "*Omni— Omni—.*"

"You better say something in Latin, quick," I told Homer. "Your protegé looks as if he's about to cry."

"If you're sure it's all right," said Homer. "You're my campaign manager."

I sighed and nodded and Homer recited the first line of Caesar's *Gallic War*.

I don't know what it was about Latin, but it sure did get Pete. While Homer recited, Pete laughed and gurgled and let my mother put the snowsuit on him.

"Did I hear you say Richard is your campaign manager?" my mother asked. "Be sure to let me know what you are running for, Homer, so I can vote for you."

"Thank you, Mrs. Sanders." Homer was shoveling the applesauce into Romulus, and Remus was staring as if he were about to die of starvation. "The truth is I have been presumptuous in assuming Richard will manage my campaign. I regret that I offered very little inspiration this morning."

"Richard did mention you were a finalist in the oratory contest."

I had done a lot more than mention it. I was proud of Homer's showing in the class competition and I'd been telling my family about it all week. In a way, I guess I thought it made me look good.

"It was a small failure, Mrs. Sanders," Homer Fink announced. "I was the school clown. You may be sure it is not a role I cherish." Homer offered a spoonful of applesauce to Remo and then he said, "I'm sorry, Richard. I didn't want to let you down."

My mother said, "I'm sure you were perfectly grand, Homer."

"It wasn't your fault the microphone was disconnected," I tried weakly and then I said, "but you just can't go through life stumbling over wires, pulling out plugs, and raving on, Homer. What good is the greatest speech in the world if nobody hears it."

Homer ladled another spoonful of applesauce into Remo, and Romy grabbed the baby spoon and waved it up and down. The applesauce flew around the room splashing against the wall and over Homer Fink.

My mother put Pete down and took the spoon from Romulus. "Some things in this world have values sufficient unto themselves, Richard. I'm sure Homer's speech was magnificent. It was the school's loss that they didn't hear it."

I didn't exactly follow that, but Homer did. He dropped his head and folded his hands in his lap. The applesauce was dripping on his jacket and I wished he would mop it up.

"Richard is right, Mrs. Sanders," Homer continued. "And that's why I'm more determined than ever to become emperor of the school. An emperor can do great good."

"There you go again," I said. "Look, you're not Pericles or Caesar and if you start that stuff it's just the disconnected microphone all over again."

"Pericles was never crowned," said Homer.

"Who cares?" Pete was rushing across the room. I caught him under the arms.

"If you boys are going to take Pete out, you'd best leave now," said my mother. "He gets colds so easily when he's overheated."

Homer Fink stood and my mother handed him a napkin. He wiped the applesauce from his face. "I wanted to tell them about life, Mrs. Sanders—that shiny, elusive element. I wanted to say we are wasting our education because we are not feeling and seeing and experiencing the rush of youth, because our hearts do not leap up."

"Of course, Homer," said my mother. To me she added, "Peter's stroller is under the front steps."

"That's why I want to run for the presidency of the school," Homer told my mother. "It's essential that we speak now. We have to let people know that we care, that we feel, that we stand triumphantly for life."

"Of course." The twins were beginning to cry for more applesauce and my mother began to feed them. "You are perfectly right, Homer."

I had Pete on my shoulder and he was calling, "*Omni—.*"

"History teaches the lessons, provides the rules and standards for achieving power," Homer went on. "And it is time the philosophers of the world were heard."

"Homer, would you mind handing me that napkin by the sink?" asked my mother.

"I call on Zeus, Jupiter—all the gods of Greece and Rome. The world has desperate need of them and they will help me," declared Homer Fink.

"I always regretted that I didn't study Greek and Latin," said my mother. "Did Richard tell you I was an English major at Goucher?"

I started to the door with Pete. I called over my shoulder, "Say, Ma, did you know Homer never went to Sunday School?"

My mother was on her way to get a washcloth to clean up the twins. "Don't keep Pete out too long," she called to me. "That's very interesting, Homer. Good luck in the election."

Pete settled down the second he saw the stroller. He smiled and said, "Me go. Me go."

"You sure do, Pete," I said and I tilted the stroller back on its rear wheels, and that made my brother scream with joy.

We cut across Lake Drive and waited for the traffic to slow down before crossing to the reservoir.

Homer Fink was by my side as we raced against the next flow of traffic.

"Ah, autumn," said Homer. "Season of mists and mellow fruitfulness."

"Open your eyes before you get a bumper wrapped around you," I told him.

"That's Keats," said Homer Fink.

We started around the gravel roadway of the reservoir and headed for the tennis courts beyond which were the open fields and the rolling hills of Druid Hill Park.

"You sure snow my mother, Homer," I said. "It's too bad the parents don't vote in our school elections."

"Will you be my campaign manager, Richard?" he asked again. "I need you."

Pete's face was flushed a rosy pink and he was bouncing up and down in the stroller. His voice was softer and less confident, but he was saying, "*Omni— Omni— Omni—*."

"If you teach my brother Latin," I told Homer Fink. "I don't think I could take this for the rest of my life."

Homer jumped with joy. He really jumped and tried to click his heels together. It attracted my attention to his shoelaces.

"The Latin alphabet has no *j* or *w*," he said to Pete. And I said, "Hold the stroller, Homer. I'll tie your shoes."

8

WE RACED THE STROLLER down the hill across the lawn and started past the tennis courts. The only people on the courts were an older man in long white ducks and white sweater instructing a blonde-haired girl who looked our age. I pushed Pete's carriage near and heard the man say, "Eye on the ball. Bring the racket back. Follow through." Homer Fink pressed his face against the metal screen enclosing the court.

"Let's listen," he urged me. "It's a lesson."

"You'll never learn tennis that way, Homer," I said. "You have to play."

"I'll master the principles," said Homer.

Pete was popping up and down in the stroller and I had to hold fast to keep it balanced. I decided to unhook him and let him roam.

Homer watched the man in white and his student. He bit his lower lip and screwed up his face. Then he took a step back from the screen and tried to imitate the teacher's movements. I play tennis sometimes with my father and I could see right off Homer was standing wrong. He looked more as if he were playing Ping-pong.

"Stand sideways to the net," I told Homer, "and keep your feet apart."

"Shhhh," said Homer Fink. "I'm studying."

Watching a tennis lesson wasn't my idea of how to spend an afternoon, but the blonde girl was interesting. She had good form. She pulled her racket back and kept her wrist firm, but when she hit the ball it often went beyond the backcourt line.

"Good. Fine. Racket back. Eye on the ball. Follow through," the instructor repeated.

The bag of tennis balls was finally empty and the instructor and the blonde girl started to collect them. They had help. Pete managed to find the entrance to the court and he was chasing tennis balls before I could stop him. He picked one up and threw it in the direction of Homer calling, *"Omni— Omni—."*

I dashed after Pete to carry him from the court. Homer was delighted. He kept urging Pete on in Latin.

When I caught Pete I made him give the ball back. "I'm sorry," I told the girl. "I mean we wouldn't want to take time from your lesson which you are probably paying for."

"That's all right," she answered. "Milt is my cousin. He only gives me lessons in the fall when he's not too busy." She put her racket down and found an old tennis ball for Pete. By this time Homer Fink had joined us on the court. I saw him on the other side of the net introducing himself to the tennis pro.

I stood there with the blonde girl and thought of how pretty she was, but I couldn't think of anything to say.

"If you'd like to hit a few, you can borrow my racket," the girl called to Homer.

Homer asked the pro if that was all right with him. The pro checked his watch and agreed and Homer Fink dashed to our side of the net. It was all he could do to keep from tripping over his overcoat.

The girl handed Homer her racket and Homer bowed and said, "Homer Fink, your servant, ma'am."

"I'm Katrinka Nonningham," she answered. "How do you do, Homer Fink."

"I do as the gods command and as the spirit moves me," was Homer's reply and he bowed again.

It seemed to me Homer was overdoing it. But Katrinka Nonningham smiled and she didn't look like the kind of girl who smiled often. Her skin was tan as though she had been playing tennis or riding around on sailboats. She didn't wear make-up or lipstick and her long blonde hair was tied in the back with a polka-dot ribbon. I was sure she would take the ribbon off the minute she stopped playing tennis. It was Katrinka Nonningham's eyes that made me think she didn't smile a lot. They were blue but very serious. She looked directly at you as if she were waiting to hear you say something important and sincere and that if it was even the smallest lie she would know. I didn't think a girl with eyes like Katrinka Nonningham's would smile for Homer Fink.

I held Homer's coat while he tried to hit the ball back to the pro. Homer rarely came close, but that didn't discourage him. Homer approached each rally as if he were an Australian Davis Cup star ready to put away the final point that would clinch the match.

Katrinka Nonningham stood quietly and watched. Pete threw the tennis ball and chased after it. He screamed, "Me. Ball. Me. Ball."

I was thinking that I really didn't have much experience with girls. I took Cindy Walsh to a dance once and a couple of times we had dates for movies. Some of the fellows like Brian Spitzer went out with girls all the time. Brian liked to talk about it. He had been dating since he was thirteen and he let us all know he had kissed three girls already. I'd thought a lot about kissing girls, but the girls I could talk to I never wanted to kiss and when I was with the girls I wanted to kiss I couldn't think of anything to say. Homer Fink wasn't much on the subject. When I mentioned to him that Elaine Steigmar was really mature for her age, Homer said there was no visual description of Helen of Troy in the *Iliad*, but when Helen left the gates of Troy, the poet told us the old men wished they were young again.

I would have liked to say that to Katrinka Nonningham but I didn't. We watched Homer rally with the pro for about fifteen minutes and neither of us said a single word.

9

A BALD-HEADED MAN joined the tennis pro, and Homer Fink brought Katrinka Nonningham's racket back to her. We were just standing there watching Pete chase tennis balls. I couldn't talk or think clearly, but Homer Fink plunged right in, reciting poetry.

> A violet by a mossy stone
> Half hidden from the eye!
> Fair as a star, when only one
> Is shining in the sky.

Katrinka Nonningham said, "Thank you, Homer Fink." And she took her racket and put it in the case and wooden frame.

74

"We'd better be starting back. I have a lot of homework to do," I said. It was only four-thirty and at that moment I would have been happy to stay in the park for the rest of my life just looking at Katrinka Nonningham. But that was all I could think of to say.

"Who are you? Where are you from?" asked Homer. "What gods have conspired to send you to us?"

Katrinka Nonningham told us she lived on Eutaw Place and went to the Park School. That's a private school and it seemed right.

I handed Homer his overcoat and picked up Pete to carry him to the stroller.

Katrinka Nonningham had on a pink sweater with pearl-colored buttons. It was all she wore over her tennis outfit. I was thinking she must be cold, but she didn't look as if she were the least uncomfortable.

"I have it," Homer exclaimed. "You must be the golden, sweet-smelling Aphrodite who rules the hearts of men."

Katrinka Nonningham tightened the screws of her tennis press, and I latched the belts of Pete's stroller.

Pete was bouncing up and down in the stroller and calling, *"Omni— Omni—."* I guess he wanted to attract Homer's attention, which was all right with me. The truth is, I wasn't

75

exactly happy about the way Homer had taken over.

Katrinka Nonningham faced Homer and looked at him with her unsmiling blue eyes. "I don't know very much about gods and goddesses. Who is Aphrodite?"

Homer bounded forward waving his arms and filling the air with his overcoat. "The goddess of love and beauty. The daughter of Zeus and Dione." Homer went on telling us how Aphrodite rose from the sea. And then he told us about her love for Mars.

Katrinka Nonningham stood absolutely still and listened. The sun ducked behind a cloud and it seemed a lot cooler to me. I wondered why she wasn't cold and I thought of asking Homer to lend her his coat.

"Prescient," screamed Homer Fink. "I feel positively prescient." He flung his overcoat into the air. Pete was greatly impressed with the flying overcoat and I had a hard time keeping him from unzipping his snowsuit.

Katrinka Nonningham said, "What does 'prescient' mean? I have never heard that word before."

"I don't believe it. It can't be true," said Homer.

I said, "I don't know what 'prescient' means, Homer. And neither does Pete."

Katrinka Nonningham's voice was calm and quiet but impatient. "Tell us what it means."

"It comes from the Latin, *praesciens*," Homer replied. "It is a feeling more than anything else—a feeling of great promise for the future." Homer wasn't exactly satisfied with that. He thought hard a moment and then he said, "Come, let's all go up to the hill and look for Pan. Something wonderful is about to happen. I know. I have foresight. I feel prescient. Don't you feel that way too, Katinka?"

Her name was Katrinka and Homer had said it wrong, but she didn't seem to notice. "I'm not sure how I feel. I'm rarely sure of how I feel," said Katrinka Nonningham. She moved her tennis racket to her shoulder and started from the courts.

"I have to be going home too," I said. "Maybe we could look for the shepherd another day."

Homer picked up his overcoat and chased after Katrinka Nonningham. "At this moment, at this instant in history, we are within reach of a new era—a rebirth. Over that hill, beyond the field on a bluff overlooking the falls, you can experience a miracle."

Katrinka Nonningham tossed her head and the long blonde hair fell over her shoulders. I wanted very much to touch her. She looked at me. "Does your friend act this way all the time?" she asked.

"Homer Fink happens to be just about the smartest kid at P.S. 79," I told her. "If anybody can see a miracle, it's Homer."

"I would like to see a miracle," she told us. "Let's go."

I pushed Pete's stroller and Katrinka Nonningham and Homer walked beside it.

"I knew it," Homer explained. "My fortune has changed. The gods have sent me Aphrodite."

I told Homer her name again. I was afraid his wild talk might scare Katrinka away. But Homer Fink said, "No. The lady is Aphrodite. One has but to look at her to see that is true. How is your father, Aphrodite? What new disguises and devices has Zeus thought up to escape Hera?"

Katrinka Nonningham said, "My father's name is Paul. He lives in San Francisco."

"Of course, San Francisco," said Homer Fink. "Noble, playful Zeus. Did he ever tell you about the time he disguised himself as a white bull to woo Europa?"

"My father lives in San Francisco because he's separated from my mother," Katrinka Nonningham said matter-of-factly.

"Your mother would be Dione," said Homer Fink. "Julius Caesar claimed descent from

78

Dione. We could be relatives." Homer was jubilant. "It could be, Richard. Julius Caesar would be a great help in winning the school election. I am a definite possibility."

I was afraid the mention of Caesar would send Peter into the *Gallic War* again, but my brother was trying to drag his hand along the ground and he wasn't paying attention to Homer.

"We could be cousins," Homer Fink said to Katrinka Nonningham. "I'm eternally indebted to you—you have my everlasting gratitude. How would you like to head up the women's committee of Julius Caesar's campaign?"

"I've never been very interested in politics," Katrinka answered.

I said, "Katrinka doesn't go to 79, Homer. She told us before that she's a student at the Park School."

"That is nothing to the point," said Homer waving his overcoat. (After the tennis rally he'd made no effort to put it back on.) "We are advocating an idea—a concept that transcends the individual. The important thing is the idea. Your school—your Park School—is just as ripe for revolution as P.S. 79."

Katrinka Nonningham lifted her chin and looked off beyond the hill into the distance. "Thank you, but no."

I would have bet my life that there wasn't a

chance of Katrinka Nonningham changing her mind.

But Homer said, "You don't understand. I haven't told you the idea yet."

We had come to a long stretch of flat ground and off in the distance we could hear the sounds of boys playing football. Katrinka Nonningham's eyes were very clear and there was a flush about the rise of her cheekbones. I was almost ready to believe Homer Fink was right. Katrinka Nonningham could have been a goddess. I had certainly never seen a girl on earth as beautiful. "I don't like to argue and I would be no help to a revolution," she said. "You told me we were going to see a miracle. If we're not, I'm going home right now."

I felt as if the sky over Druid Hill Park was black with clouds and the air was still. I was certain we had lost her. But Homer said, "That's it—that's the whole point. We are going to see a miracle. The miracle is the reason for the revolution." Then Homer said, "Follow me."

On the way up to the hill Homer told us about the death of Pan. I was pushing Pete's stroller on the rear wheels to keep his hand from scraping the ground. I heard Homer say, "At the time of the Crucifixion a great cry swept across the ocean. 'Great Pan is dead.' There is a poem about it."

Earth outgrows the mythic fancies
Sung beside her in her youth;
And those debonaire romances
Sound but dull beside the truth.
Phoebus' chariot course is run!
Look up, poets, to the sun!
　　　Pan, Pan is dead.

"Did you write that poem?" Katrinka asked Homer.

Hardly hearing her question, Homer went on. "It's ridiculous. A graceful lie," said Homer Fink. "Great Pan isn't dead. He's just been sleeping. Isn't that right, Richard? Didn't we see him?"

"I'd rather you wouldn't bring me into this," I said softly.

"Don't you believe Homer?" Katrinka Nonningham asked me. "I thought he was your friend."

I could see she was very impressed. I guess she thought Homer had made up the poem just like that—one, two, three. She really went for Homer's poetry.

I shrugged and said, "Homer's my friend. We walk to school together every day."

"Richard saw Pan," Homer told Katrinka. "And you and Peter are going to see him too."

We waited on the hill overlooking Jones Fall for fifteen minutes and nothing happened. It was close to five o'clock and it was growing dark. I let Pete out of the stroller and he was having a great time rolling down the hill. Homer told Katrinka Nonningham and me to be very quiet and think. I wanted to ask him what he would suggest we think about. But there was an expression on Homer's face that indicated that if I didn't know I shouldn't be there.

Homer was picking blades of grass and piling them into small stacks and Katrinka Nonningham was lying on the ground with her chin resting in her hand and eyes closed. I suggested Katrinka use Homer's coat as a blanket. He wasn't wearing it and I could see she was beginning to feel cold even if she didn't mention it.

I made up my mind not to be the first to speak. I wasn't thinking about Pan or any of the Greek gods. I was wondering if Pete was going to catch cold because we were out so long, and if my mother was going to be sore because I came back after dark, and if the miracle failed, would I ever see Katrinka again. I thought about all those things for a while and then I just settled upon thinking that this was ridiculous. There was no Pan—only a shepherd in Druid Hill Park and it was very unlikely that he would be grazing his sheep at twilight.

"You're not praying hard enough," Homer said suddenly. "Let's burn incense." He was on his feet clapping his hands and bowing furiously. "'Heap the shrine of luxury and pride with incense kindled at the muse's flame,'" he said.

Pete was halfway up the hill. He was stumbling and falling all over himself, but he got a big kick out of Homer Fink's hand-clapping. Pete started clapping his hands too. It didn't help his balance. Every time he clapped he fell.

"Gather pine cones," Homer directed Katrinka Nonningham. "Do you hear my command, maiden? Get thee pine cones for our offering to Pan."

Katrinka Nonningham sat up and folded her arms over her knees. I could tell she wasn't used to boys ordering her around.

"Gather ye pine cones," Homer said impatiently. "I command thee, maiden. Do not tarry."

I said, "I think Homer wants to start a fire or something, Katrinka. We might find some pine cones in the woods. I'll help."

Homer raised one hand and held the other over his heart. "You there, Hephaestus," he said to me, "Keeper of the flame and guardian of the forge—ignite the bier."

I said, "Listen, Homer, it's not exactly safe to start fires in Druid Hill Park. Maybe we'd better forget it."

Homer raised both hands toward the sky and faced the direction from which we had seen the shepherd appear several weeks ago. "Oh, great god Pan," he chanted, "your servants await thee. Come to us and play your pipes of reed. Let us rejoice in melodies as sweet as the nightingale's song."

Pete had managed to crawl near the top of the hill. We saw Homer with his hands outstretched. My brother laughed and raised his hands too and said, "Me. Indian. Me. Indian." It wasn't exactly what you would expect from a two-and-a-half-year-old who was learning Caesar's *Gallic War*, but television had gotten to Pete before Homer Fink discovered him.

Katrinka Nonningham stood up, looked at Homer and then at me and then at Pete crawling up the hill. Suddenly Katrinka Nonningham was dashing off to the woods to look for pine cones. It wasn't every day somebody invited her to burn incense to the gods, and I guess she decided to go right along with it.

I found some small sticks to use as kindling and built a square with lots of air space. Homer was chanting in Greek and Pete was echoing with an Indian war whoop.

When Katrinka returned with two pine

cones Homer was satisfied. He directed me to start the fire.

"It isn't that easy, Homer," I said. "If you don't have a match, I'll have to rub two sticks together. That takes time."

I was a Cub Scout for four years and I made it all the way to Webelos. I spent two years in the Boy Scouts besides, but the truth is I never really started a fire by rubbing sticks together. Somebody always had matches.

My wrists were sore and my fingers numb, but I kept rubbing the sticks for all I was worth. If Katrinka Nonningham hadn't been with us I would have given up and tried to talk Homer out of burning incense. But Katrinka had a bright dewy look about her eyes. I could see the idea really got to her and I didn't want to be the one to let her down.

The sun was very low, and off in the distance the park was black. There were long shadows of trees and we could hear the first sounds of night animals. Homer and I were concentrating on rubbing the sticks and Katrinka was holding Pete to keep him from knocking down our bier.

None of us spoke and I was beginning to feel a flush of shame for failing Katrinka. I was just about positive I could never get a spark from the two sticks.

And then we heard the first, faint notes of a song. It seemed to come from the other side of the hill. I dropped the sticks and none of us moved.

"Ah, the pipes of reed," exclaimed Homer. "Pan is coming."

I saw Katrinka Nonningham shiver.

"You'd better put on Homer's coat," I told her. "You'll get pneumonia."

"Silence," Homer ordered me. "He's coming. Pan has returned. Rejoice, oh ye hills and myrtle bows and woodland nymphs—the shepherd's god is returning."

I listened attentively. There was no doubt that the music was getting closer. But it didn't sound at all like a pipe or any kind of instrument. I thought I heard a man's voice. He was singing a song and I was sure I recognized the word "glorious." There were other words to the song, but the man's voice was indistinct and it was difficult to understand exactly what he was singing.

Homer Fink heard it too. "Answer with me," he directed us. "Repeat—'glorious, glorious.'"

"What about the fire?" I said. "Should we forget all about burning incense?"

Homer didn't answer. He raised his hands to the heavens again, chanted in Greek, and repeated, "Glorious, glorious."

Katrinka Nonningham stood by his side, repeating with him, "Glorious—glorious."

I was ready to greet Pan. I was wondering about his goat horns and looking forward to seeing his hoofs. I could feel my knees trembling.

The singing was more distinct. It was obvious "the piper," as Homer called him, had heard our refrain and was coming to join us.

The words were very clear if not inspiring. The man was singing "glorious" all right. And the next verse went:

One keg of beer for the four of us.
Glory be to God that there are no more of us,
Because one of us could drink it all alone.

We saw him wandering about the base of the hill. He was a jovial fat old man with a beer bottle in one hand and a shopping bag in the other. When he walked, he weaved from side to side. It was all he could do to stay on his feet.

"Do you want me to run after him and ask him for a match?" I asked Homer Fink.

"It's not Pan. You promised us a miracle and all we've seen is a drunk, fat old man," cried Katrinka Nonningham. "I hate you, Homer Fink." Katrinka took off Homer's coat and threw it down. Then she kicked at the sticks we had built for the fire and picked up her tennis racket and ran away. I was sure she was crying.

"There goes your women's committee," I said to Homer, and I was feeling lonely and empty already.

Homer Fink was more interested in the old man. He stared after him. There was an expression about Homer's face as if he had just seen Zeus himself riding through the heavens on his golden chariot, gathering thunderbolts.

"I give up," I said. I picked up Pete and put him back in his stroller. "If we hurry we can get out of the park before night."

"A miracle," said Homer Fink. "Richard, we have witnessed a second miracle."

We started down the hill and headed toward home. "Katrinka Nonningham didn't think so," I said. "Didn't you think she was really beautiful, Homer? Wouldn't you like to see her again?"

"Never fear," Homer Fink assured me. "Aphrodite will join us. I have merely to explain that she was witness to the coming of Silenus —brother of Pan and a good friend of Bacchus." Homer paused and then he said with great assurance, "Tomorrow at four o'clock, the B. and O. terminal. Even Caesar didn't cross the Rubicon twice in one day."

10

Passenger trains don't run from the B. and O.'s Mt. Royal terminal any more, but the clock works and we could see it from the west windows of P.S. 79 or when we were going to gym or traveling to and from school. The gray brick of the clock tower is majestic compared to the schoolhouse, and I have always thought of it as a part of the school rather than a city landmark. I looked to the big hands to tell me how much longer I would have to wait for recess or lunch or the school bell.

A great stairway leads down to the terminal, and there is a driveway that once served the cars and taxis carrying passengers. Few cars park in the spaces flanking the station now, and rarely do we see people going and coming. Sometimes in the spring, when we were in the lower grades, we would play step ball on the staircase. It is handy for ruling off bases or sitting and watching the birds that roost and shelter under the tower.

After lunch period the next day, I heard Homer Fink say to Phillip Moore, "I'll be expecting you after school—under the clock."

We were in the schoolyard and Homer started to the gate. Ninth-graders were allowed to make brief visits to the candy store or to buy ice cream from the vendor on the corner. That day I heard another reason for leaving the schoolyard. Mr. Muncrief was guarding the gate and Homer told him, "I have some thinking to do, sir, and I think better when I walk. I'm sure you are acquainted with the peripatetic philosophers."

The collar of Homer's tweed coat was rolled under and Mr. Muncrief adjusted it. He patted Homer lightly on the back and stared after him, concentrating on the cuffs of Homer's pants which barely missed catching under the heels of his shoes.

Homer didn't show for afternoon classes, and at three-thirty when Phillip Moore, Brian Spitzer, and I started to the terminal I said, "I hope nothing has happened to Homer. It's not like him to play hookey."

"We have an appointment," said Phillip Moore. "I know Homer wouldn't have made the date if he didn't intend to keep it."

"I wonder what Fink is up to now," said Brian. "Remember when he had us all sign a petition against cutting up dogs at hospitals?"

"Homer is an antivivisectionist," Phillip tried to explain to Brian. But I didn't listen closely. I was thinking neither Phillip nor Brian knew that Homer was going to announce he was running for the presidency of the school. We started across the island of Hoffman Street where Trudy Deal and Patty Esposito were waiting for the bus. Considering that Phillip was an obvious candidate and that Brian was no fan of Homer's, I decided to have the others join us.

"We're going to hear Homer Fink make a speech," I called. "Want to come along?"

The memory of Homer's riotous show in the auditorium was fresh in their minds. By the time we'd reached Mt. Royal, Patty had a dozen of her classmates with her.

Brian wasn't making out so well in his argument with Phillip Moore and he welcomed an opportunity to change the subject. "I'll bet Homer Fink wants us to go on a sit-down strike on the railroad tracks or something like that," said Brian. "Remember how once in class he made a long speech about it?"

"Homer was talking about Mahatma Gandhi," said Phillip.

"Hey, fellows," Brian Spitzer called to a group nearby. "Homer Fink is going on a hunger strike. B. and O. Railroad terminal. Four o'clock."

Several minutes after we arrived, the area surrounding the B. and O. terminal was jammed. Not only was there a mob of students from P.S. 79 but I recognized a dozen fellows from the neighboring Latin School and a group from the Bryn Mawr School for Girls.

The crush was terrific. Brian Spitzer was shouting, "The tracks. Out to the tracks. Fink's hunger strike begins at sunset."

I heard one of the girls from the eighth grade say, "Isn't this exciting. Homer Fink thinks of everything."

Homer may have been thinking of everything, but it was past four and I was hoping Homer's thoughts included an appearance at the terminal.

By four-fifteen Trudy Deal was stretched out on a bench rolling her eyes and fanning herself with a Latin notebook.

"Stand back," commanded Marvin Bloom, and he started shoving kids away from the bench.

Trudy Deal liked to create a crisis, and Marvin Bloom enjoyed nothing better than an excuse to throw his weight around.

"Water . . . water before I faint," whined Trudy.

Marvin boomed, "Get the kid a drink before I bust somebody."

Little Louie Bannerman weaved through the crowd and made his way to Trudy. "If you're feeling faint sit up, loosen your collar, and place your head between your knees."

"Stop horsing around," Marvin told Louie. "This kid is in no shape for calisthenics."

Louie reminded Marvin that he was the son of a practicing physician. But Marvin Bloom insisted all Trudy needed was for everybody to stand back. After a brief announcement to that effect Marvin flung his one hundred and forty pounds into the crowd, shoulders down, arms bent and raised. He must have had visions of clearing the line for Lenny Moore of the football Colts. Patty Esposito finally slowed Marvin by hitting him with her science textbook.

I was beginning to fear a riot if Homer didn't arrive. I was also considering the possibilities of Homer speaking, once he did appear. The pavement around the terminal was beginning to look more and more like the floor of a political convention, complete with absent candidates.

Phillip Moore tried to get the crowd under control. Standing on a bench, he warned about fire hazards and keeping calm. When that didn't work, Phillip started singing the school song. Some of the boys and girls thought that was a fine idea—they were in the glee club.

Nobody else sang. Not that we don't have school spirit. You have to be practically a Richard Tucker or Joan Sutherland to sing 79's Alma Mater, "Great Old Lafayette." I never understood the words until my senior year. I always thought we were singing, "Gray Old Lafayette."

There was a lot of speculation as to what Homer Fink was up to. I heard one boy say, "Fink hasn't eaten in three days. He'll never take another bite until the school board outlaws homework."

"Did you hear about Homer Fink?" an eighth-grader announced. "He's sitting on the B. and O. tracks, and freight trains are backed up to Havre de Grace."

"Fink is organizing a march on City Hall," said another. "He wants a four-day school week and more holidays."

I don't know who started the rumor, but it swept around the terminal. "Homer Fink is standing on the clock tower."

Louie Bannerman had brought Trudy Deal around by then. She was sitting up and breathing deep and Louie was suggesting that she get some fresh air and rest. When Trudy heard that Homer was on the clock tower she screamed, "Stop him. He'll jump."

That was the cue for a retreat to the steps where we would have a view of the clock tower. A moment before, everyone had been determined to get as close to the train tracks as possible. But now the students made a dash to the steps.

As Phillip Moore and I joined the others, Phillip said, "I wonder what Homer intended to announce."

I was ready to explain, but we were interrupted by a great cry from the students. They were massed in mackinaws and overcoats, loafers and saddle shoes, braids and Beatlecuts. With their schoolbooks under their arms they roared, "Fink. Fink. Fink."

Those nearest the terminal were staring at the tower and momentarily I believed Homer was standing by the big clock. I prayed that Homer Fink had no delusions of wearing winged sandals. He had told me the story of Perseus, and it occurred to me that he may have been as convinced of meeting Hermes as he was of our encounters with Pan and Silenus.

Phillip and I dashed around the crowd. (There was no chance of breaking through them.) We stationed ourselves on the highest steps in order to have the best view.

A girl screamed, "He's up there. I saw him."

"Send for the cops and the fire department," advised another.

A boy who watched a lot of war stories on television explained, "You can't see Homer because he's camouflaged by the brick."

All eyes were on the clock tower and again the chant began: "Fink. Fink. Fink."

I cupped my hands over my eyes and stared hard. I examined every foot of the clock tower until I was absolutely positive Homer Fink wasn't there.

"It's an illusion," Phillip Moore said to me. "Unless Homer has already jumped."

"Homer Fink wouldn't even do a forward somersault—much less jump from a tower," I told Phillip.

It was then I heard a dog bark and in the next moment I felt a nip at my heels.

"Get away from me, Argus," I complained and I swung my foot to throw him off.

"It's him. It's Homer Fink," a girl screamed. And all eyes turned to the head of the stairs where Homer Fink stood, his hands pressed deep into the pockets of his oversized overcoat. Homer's face was flushed and his hair was askew. It was obvious he had been walking for a long time and I knew he had traveled far —at least as far as the Park School—for by his side was Katrinka Nonningham.

"Homer Fink has returned from the dead,"

cried Trudy Deal. "I think I'm going to faint."

"It's a ghost," declared a seventh-grader.

"Who is he, anyway?" asked a fellow from the Latin School.

The reply came from the chorus: "Fink. Fink. Fink."

Homer held his hand up, signaling for quiet. He seemed not the least surprised by the great crowd or the enthusiasm of the greeting. "I have been reading Plato and thinking hard," Homer Fink announced. "And I have concluded I am a wolf."

I didn't have to be a professional politician to know that this was no time for Homer to make a speech on Plato. I hurried to the front of the crowd and with Argus still yelping at my heels, I said, "Fellow students, classmates, friends, we all know that in the next few weeks the students of P.S. 79 will be called upon to elect a president of our student council. We will be looking for a boy who can express our opinions and create programs to satisfy our needs—a boy who is exciting and inspiring. A boy who is loyal. A boy who is helpful—" I was joined in the recitation of the Boy Scout qualities. "Friendly . . . courteous . . . kind . . . obedient . . . cheerful . . . thrifty. . . ."

There was a tug at my sleeve and I heard Homer say, "No more 'boy-who,' please, Richard." Homer went on to explain that he intended to point out the beast in our nature. He must have tried this speech on Katrinka Nonningham because she told me, "It has to be said."

The students were chanting Homer's name and cheering. We had built to the climax and I knew we shouldn't delay. The stage was set for Homer Fink to sweep into office without opposition. All he had to do was say something simple and to the point. But Homer was primed for philosophy and I had to discourage him.

"Let's hear it," I urged the crowd. "Who is he? What's the name of the 'boy-who'?"

While the crowd was letting off steam, I talked to Homer. "Tell them you think we should have a varsity football team," I advised. "Say that. And nothing more."

Argus had hold of my trouser cuff and I gave him a gentle boot to drive him away.

Katrinka Nonningham dashed to the rescue, picking up Argus and holding him in her arms. She didn't seem to be the kind of girl who would make a big fuss over animals. I guessed Homer had told her about Ulysses and how his dog Argus had recognized him when he returned from his wanderings.

What happened after that would make Machiavelli roll over in his grave. I don't remember how he started or what made him stop, but Homer Fink gave a long speech. He wanted us to think about the meaning of life and the purpose of government.

It was dark when Homer finally concluded. He promised to talk more later and mentioned a vigorous campaign of ideas.

Katrinka Nonningham was sitting on the steps petting Argus and Phillip Moore was standing in front of Homer looking up at him as if the message was coming right from Olympus. A couple of fellows from the Latin School stayed, but everyone else went home.

As we started back up the steps Phillip said, "I was interested in your thoughts concerning the responsibility of government. It doesn't seem to me we talk about that nearly enough."

"It would be a big help if we had one person in each homeroom working for Homer's election," I suggested to Phillip.

"I've never heard a boy admit he was part beast," said Katrinka Nonningham. "Homer is right. We have to control our nature so that we are free for higher purposes. I get so bored with boys trying to kiss me all the time."

"I intend to discuss all kinds of ideas in this campaign," said Homer Fink. And then turning to me he said, "Thanks for getting my constituents together, Richard. I hope we gave them something to think about."

11

MOTHER WAS IN THE KITCHEN feeding the twins and Pete was banging pots together in his playpen. My father had a cup of coffee and the *Evening Sun* in front of him on the kitchen table. He was reading a column aloud. It had to do with something going on in Washington. My father must have thought it was funny, I heard him say, "Did you hear that, Lil? This is a parody of a Presidential press conference."

"Do you think you could take Pete downtown for shoes on Saturday?" answered my mother. "I have an appointment with Dr. Smith for the twins' shots in the afternoon."

My father laughed at something he read. "You must listen to this, Lil. It'll do you good."

Although my mother nodded, she couldn't smile. She had a diaper pin in her mouth. My father had to move the coffee cup and paper from the table to make room for my brother, Remus.

"I went to the Hopkins with Russ Baker in '46," my father told me.

I said, "That's great. Was he an all American lacrosse star?"

"Not exactly. He's a syndicated columnist who appears in the *Sun*." I could see by my father's expression that I had discouraged him.

As soon as the diaper pin was out of her mouth, my mother said, "Richard could use a new pair of crepe soles too. And don't let them sell you the exact size—a half size larger, please."

"Homer Fink is running for the presidency of our school," I told my father. "I'm his campaign manager."

My father put down the paper. "That's fine, Richard. No better time to start."

My father was a lawyer and he had once been active in politics. I remembered the year before the twins were born when we went around the neighborhood distributing handbills and hanging up signs for a friend of his who was running for the State Assembly. I don't recall the friend's name. After the election I guess you couldn't have found very many people in the city of Baltimore who remembered him any better than I did.

That was the last time my father was involved in politics. I had heard him say many times that he wished he had the time to do some real campaigning.

"We had our first rally this afternoon," I went on. "It was terrific, but a flop."

"Did you do all of your homework?" my mother asked.

I told her I had.

My father took a cigar from his pocket and lit it. "So you're in politics and Homer Fink is your man."

"Homer wants to be the president of the school," I explained. "He's heard the call."

Pete must have recognized Homer's name. He banged a saucepan against a small fryer and shouted, "*Omni—.*"

"Homer's teaching Pete Latin," I told my dad.

My father winked. "I'm not sure I approve of making deals."

Remus sneezed and Romulus was gurgling. "Why don't you gentlemen retire to the living room for your talk," suggested my mother. "It's much more comfortable."

Waving the cigar smoke from Remus' head, my father said, "Come along, Richard. A kitchen is no place for a smoke-filled room." He led me to the basement and opened an old trunk. There were bumper stickers and blotters with the name of the candidate he had supported and a large clip-board that my father dusted and gave me. "This clip-board will come in handy for your campaign memos," he said.

We sat on orange crates near the boiler and my father told me how to organize a political campaign. He talked about "communication" and ways to "get your message to the voter." I could see he was eager to talk. Politics meant a lot to my father and I guess if that fellow who had run for State Assembly decided to try again my father would have been very tempted to help him. (I still couldn't remember the candidates' names even five minutes after seeing them spelled out all over the bumper stickers and blotters.)

"Government is everybody's responsibility," declared my father. "We can't leave it to the professional politicians to run the country."

I tried to explain that there weren't any professional politicians at P.S. 79. The most popular students in the school were usually elected. But my father wanted to tell me all about machines and reformers.

The way I understood it, the machine politicians controlled government because they gave away jobs and did people favors and had workers keeping in touch with the voters. Machine politicians wanted things to stay pretty much the way they were, according to my father. And it took reformers such as the fellow he had supported for State Assembly to bring in new ideas and make people aware of what was going on, whether they liked it or not.

"That's Homer Fink all over," I told my dad. "He's bringing in ideas all the time."

"Good for Homer Fink," said my father. "And what is it Homer wants to reform?"

I hadn't really thought about that before. I rocked on the orange crate and studied the boiler a while and then I said, "I guess when you really come right down to it, all Homer Fink wants to reform is the world."

My father chomped on his cigar and was quiet.

"That's about it, Dad," I said and I stood. "How about a quick game of Ping-pong?"

We didn't say anything more about politics. I caught my father twice on easy backhands and he missed the table with four slams. I won 21–19, which was really something because I only beat him once before. That was the night before the twins were born and we were killing time while waiting for the call from the hospital.

12

THE DAY BEFORE THE nominating assembly, a large sign appeared on the fence between the girls' and boys' yards. It announced: JOIN THE PLAN FOR BANNERMAN. There was room for signatures and although it wasn't official, lots of students wrote their names on the sign.

Homer thought it was a great idea and I had to convince him not to write a message encouraging Little Louie.

It was during lunch hour and Homer and I were standing near a group playing wall ball. "At last we know the enemy," I said to Homer. "Little Louie is very popular in his class and you can be sure he'll give us a tough time on issues. We have to start hitting him and hitting him hard."

"Little Louie is my friend," said Homer. "Let's find him and hear what he's thinking."

"It may be a better idea to save our energy and try to develop something that will attract as much attention as Louie's sign," I suggested.

Homer clasped his hands behind his back. "We must find out all about Louie's campaign plans."

Homer wasn't suggesting undercover work. He was expressing curiosity. "It doesn't work that way in politics," I explained. "Candidates don't share ideas with each other. They try to come up with a better platform than their opponent so they can win more votes."

"Our campaign will be different," Homer told me. "Louie is welcome to my ideas. I hope he'll stand with us and search for justice, which comprises in it all virtue. *Justitia in se virtutem complectitur omnen.*"

A ball bounced our way. Homer made a great flourish of trying to catch it, but it rolled through his legs. I backed him up, caught it, and returned it to the players. "I've been meaning to talk to you about that, Homer," I said. "I was hoping we could explain our platform in English and try to make it more specific."

"There is nothing more specific than truth, Richard," said Homer Fink. "And the time to pursue it is now when we are young enough to be free and old enough to be strong."

"You better talk to Little Louie," I said. "A bipartisan policy on truth and justice could be just what we need to clear the deck and get down to the issue of the noise in the cafeteria."

We found Little Louie perched on the shoulders of Marvin Bloom. He was looking over the fence into the girls' yard and we could hear him saying, "Hi, girls. Vote for Bannerman if you want a school prom."

"We had better have some signs circulated this afternoon," I said to Homer.

Homer dashed across the yard and offered his hand to his opponent. "I'm sure we will have a spirited campaign, Louie," he said. "I gather you're addressing yourself to the ladies."

"You bet your Vitalis we are." Marvin Bloom gave Louie's legs a tug. "And we aren't bringing in any ringers like that blonde who was baby-sitting for your dog."

"Katrinka is my friend," Homer answered. "She isn't going to vote."

From his lofty height Little Louie warned, "I may be forced by conscience to make an issue of outside assistance."

I was about to interrupt and cover Homer by telling them Katrinka was *my* friend, but

107

Homer changed the subject. "How do you see the position of women in our society?" he asked Louie.

"I see them as votes," was Louie's answer.

Then Marvin Bloom said, "A prom wouldn't be much without girls."

"My view is women have the same capacities as men," said Homer.

"By 'capacities' Homer Fink means girls are as good as boys," Louie Bannerman announced to the boys on our side of the fence. "They can do anything boys can do."

"Are you nuts or something?" said Marvin Bloom. "Show me a girl who can pass like Johnny Unitas or throw a punch like Floyd Patterson."

"That's not the full measure of an individual's ability," Homer tried to explain. "My point is that women should not be discouraged from taking full and useful places in society. It's all in Plato."

"Nuts to Plato," a boy called from the crowd. "He could talk because he didn't manage the Orioles."

Comfortably seated on Marvin's shoulders, Little Louie leaned on the fence. Even though we couldn't see her, I could hear Trudy Deal ohing and ahing in response to Louie's announcement about the prom. Some of the girls were squealing in that way they have that made me doubt the truth of Homer's statement.

"If you elect me, I will press for a five-piece band," Louie was saying. He lowered his voice and while Homer Fink was defending the merits of a woman president to the boys, Little Louie Bannerman was whispering to the girls, "I'm going to fight to make sure this prom is a formal, whether the boys like it or not."

With Louie Bannerman winning the girls' vote and Homer simultaneously discouraging the boys' vote, I knew what my father meant by a communications problem.

"Quick, Homer, up on my shoulders," I said.

It took some urging, and Phillip Moore had to give him a boost before Homer finally agreed. By this time all the boys in the yard had gathered around us. I heard a voice from the rear of the crowd say, "Fink and Bannerman are going to have a horse fight."

Addressing the girls on the other side of the fence, Homer received a much warmer response to his theories on women's rights. I asked Little Louie if it was true that he wanted the boys to wear tuxedos to the prom. Louie said he was going to appoint a committee to investigate that, but Marvin Bloom bounced him vigorously on his shoulders and announced, "I'm not wearing a monkey suit for anybody."

I was beginning to feel we had the communications problem licked when a whistle blew and Mr. Muncrief's voice demanded, "What is the meaning of this?"

"A horse fight," the voice from the rear repeated.

"I will give those boys detention. Who are they?" Mr. Muncrief rushed toward us. "What are their names?"

There is a difference between "being kept in after school" and "detention." If we talk in class without permission or fail to do our homework or chew gum and are caught before we can stick it under our seats, the teacher will ask us to stay after school.

Detention is reserved for students with whom the teacher is unable to cope in class or as a punishment for creating a major school disorder. Detention is noted on our report cards and constant offenders are asked to bring their parents to school. You didn't exactly have to be a Franklin Delano Roosevelt to realize that an afternoon of detention was no way to begin a career in school politics.

I had to make one of those on-the-spot decisions required of men in public life. Either Homer would stay perched and share the dishonor of detention with his opponent or risk a more severe penalty by making a bid to escape.

There was no time for discussion. "Over the fence," I advised my candidate. And with a quick lift from me, Homer Fink went flying over the fence into the girls' yard.

Little Louie Bannerman was not above borrowing that idea. But strong as he was, Marvin Bloom's reflexes were a little slow.

Homer had disappeared into the girls' side of the yard and Louie Bannerman was straddling the fence when Mr. Muncrief arrived in the center of the crowd.

"Stop, right where you are," the assistant principal directed Little Louie. "What kind of Peeping Tom stunt are you up to, Louis Bannerman? I'll see you at detention this afternoon. As for the rest of you boys—I'm ashamed —ashamed of all of you!"

13

HOMER FINK did not appear in class that afternoon.

I had arranged with Patty Esposito and a group from her class to distribute "THINK WITH FINK" signs after school. We met in the library where I learned that Trudy Deal had been the last person to talk with Homer.

Trudy explained there had been great excitement in the girls' yard when Homer arrived. The girls protected Homer from the teacher monitoring the yard and shielded him when they lined up to return to classes after recess.

"We got as far as the girls' washroom," Trudy explained. "Then Homer wandered off."

"Wandered off where?" Phillip Moore wanted to know. "There's no way for Homer to have re-entered the school without having been seen by a teacher."

"Maybe he was caught," Patty suggested. "Homer could have been sent to Mr. Muncrief's office."

"He could be there right now." Trudy's eyes filled with tears. You would have thought Homer was a prisoner at Sing Sing.

"There's only one way to find out," I said "I'll look."

I started down the deserted hall and passed the library where Dr. Creel sat reading a thick book. Mr. Bowen was at the blackboard in the science lab. With colored crayons he was drawing a picture of a frog for his biology class which met the next morning. Miss Pierce was busy marking history tests.

My shoes echoed down the hall and as I came closer to Mr. Muncrief's office I walked on tiptoe. It wouldn't be easy to explain my presence to the assistant principal, but I had to take the chance. If Homer Fink had been caught in the girls' washroom, his campaign manager should be the first to know.

When I was several feet from the assistant principal's door, I heard Mr. Muncrief's voice. I stopped and listened. "It's only natural, Louis. All boys have a curiosity about girls. But that's

113

not the way we express it," Mr. Muncrief was saying. "It may be that we are a little old-fashioned separating the girls' playground from the boys'," he continued. "But in many ways it's an advantage to you young fellows to be able to run and play ball and not have to consider bumping into or injuring the girls. Have you ever looked at it that way? Did you consider that, Louis?"

"No, sir." From the sound of his voice I knew Bannerman didn't have the least idea of what Mr. Muncrief was driving at.

"You see girls every day in class, don't you?"

"Yes, sir."

"And they're not really that different, are they? After all they have two eyes, two ears, a nose, a mouth—just the same as you or I."

"That's true," Little Louie agreed.

"Now, I wouldn't try to pretend to you—a doctor's son—that boys and girls are exactly alike. No indeed, I wouldn't," said Mr. Muncrief. "Why, for all I know you've been poking around in your dad's books and seeing a thing or two that might be news to me. And if that's agreeable to your parents, it is certainly acceptable to us."

"Excuse me, sir. What books?" Louie asked suddenly.

"Your dad's books—his medical books," said Mr. Muncrief. "Come along now, Louis, I'm not going to punish you. There's certainly nothing to be ashamed of. Surely a boy who would climb on the fence to look into the girls' yard would be tempted to browse through a medical book—if only to see the pictures."

"I looked up 'impetigo' once," said Louie Bannerman. "You treat it with sulfonamides or penicillin."

"I'm sure you do," said Mr. Muncrief. There was a long pause and then I heard Mr. Muncrief say to Louie Bannerman, "Suppose you tell me, Louis, in your own words exactly why you were on the fence looking into the girls' yard?"

Little Louie was a politician all the way. Without the slightest hesitation he announced, "No comment, sir."

When Mr. Muncrief started to talk there was a forced cheerfulness to his voice. "You know what you and I are going to do tomorrow at recess, Louis? We are going to organize group calisthenics. How would you like that? We'll do push-ups and deep-knee bends. Some fine, exhausting exercises to help build strong bodies and sound minds. After a half hour, why, we won't give two hoots about the girls' yard. Youngsters your age need an activity to keep them occupied. It's just that simple."

There was the sound of footsteps coming down the hall and I knew I had to get away

115

fast. Starting down the steps to the basement, I looked over my shoulder and saw Mr.
Aberdenally. The school custodian was headed
to Mr. Muncrief's office with a broomstick in
one hand and an empty mousetrap in the
other.

"I looked all over the yard. Homer's not
there," Phillip Moore reported.

Patty Esposito had to be getting home for a
music lesson and the others had long since de-
parted. Phillip and I sat on the curb and tried
to consider other possibilities.

Phillip suggested we call Homer's house. I volunteered a dime and we made the call from
the drugstore. Mrs. Fink hadn't seen her son
since he left for school in the morning.

"Homer must be around the school area,"
Phillip insisted. "Either he's in the girls' locker
room or concealed in the yard or hiding out
in the cafeteria."

We agreed we would need a girl to check
the girls' locker and Phillip thought it would
be a good idea to get in touch with Katrinka.
I wasn't going to argue with that. We looked
up "Nonningham" in the telephone book and
discovered Katrinka had her own phone. When
I told Katrinka that Homer Fink had disappeared, she said she was on her way.

While we were waiting for Katrinka, Phillip
Moore told me some of his ideas for the cam-

paign. The way he saw it, we should be introducing "major issues." Phillip wanted to get the students talking about the emerging nations of Africa and Asia and fighting poverty and things like that.

"I'm sure if Homer Fink applied himself he could make really important contributions to solving these problems," said Phillip.

I told him what I had learned outside the door to Mr. Muncrief's office. It seemed to me that if Little Louie Bannerman was responsible for the boys doing calisthenics during recess, that would prove a far more effective issue for us than Homer's position on world peace.

Katrinka Nonningham arrived in a taxicab. She was wearing a polo coat and had on tennis shoes and lacy black stockings. "Where is he? What happened to Homer?"

"He's probably all right," I said. "But we need somebody to search the girls' locker."

It wasn't exactly my idea of an exciting afternoon date, but Katrinka was anxious to get to it.

Down the hall from the girls' room was the kitchen. Phillip and I made a thorough search of that area. The freezer was locked and so was the refrigerator. I couldn't remember the names of any Norse gods, but I prayed silently that Homer hadn't decided to conceal himself in either of those places.

We met Katrinka by the door leading to the girls' yard. "I'm sure Homer Fink has made himself invisible. When he's ready, he'll return."

Phillip Moore said, "You don't seem to realize the gravity of the world situation, Katrinka. We need Homer now."

I suppose Katrinka and Phillip could have gone on discussing whether Homer was more valuable as a deity or as a statesman, but we heard voices echoing in the basement.

"Steady. Steady as you go," Mr. Muncrief was saying. "If there's a mouse we'll find it."

"I saw that mouse go up the riser," Mr. Aberdenally, the custodian, replied. "I tell you he's in your office somewhere."

The assistant principal's voice came closer. "It is much more likely that a mouse would be nesting in the basement."

"That's him. I'm sure that's Homer." I had to grasp Katrinka Nonningham's arm to keep her from starting in the direction of the voices.

"That's Mr. Muncrief, the assistant principal of our school," I told her. "And if he finds us here, Homer will have to start looking for a new campaign team. We have to hide."

"Don't you remember? Didn't Homer teach you anything? The Greek gods change their form all the time."

118

"Homer's too small to disguise himself as Mr. Muncrief or Mr. Aberdenally. Their clothes would never fit him."

"Homer's not a man," Katrinka announced. "Homer Fink must—be—the—mouse."

"I doubt it," said Phillip Moore. "I really don't believe transmigration is possible."

"Behind the garbage cans," I insisted. "They're coming."

We darted around the dishwashing machine and made our way between the racks of cups and bowls. The cans were lined up in a semi-circle and we crouched behind them.

"I'm sure I'm right. We don't have to hide. There's nothing to be ashamed of," said Katrinka.

"Keep your head down," I whispered.

Phillip Moore hunched into a tight corner and Katrinka and I huddled beside him. Mr. Muncrief and Mr. Aberdenally came closer.

"The first time in thirty-five years a mouse in my school," the custodian said. "I tell you it is an evil sign—bad luck."

"Nonsense," Mr. Muncrief consoled him. "It is no such thing. We just have to keep the cafeteria a little cleaner, that's all."

"It's those children," said Mr. Aberdenally. "They throw crumbs and food all over the floor. It's a wonder we didn't have mice long ago. No table manners and too much to eat.

The only trouble with this school is those spoiled brats." There was the sound of Mr. Aberdenally's broom slamming against the floor. "Thought I had her. Must have been a shadow."

"Take it easy. Don't get yourself all worked up," Mr. Muncrief advised Mr. Aberdenally. "Remember, it may be a mouse to you but it's some creature's daughter."

I put my arm around Katrinka Nonningham's shoulder to help her keep her balance. A wisp of her hair brushed against my cheek.

"Plato is right," I confessed, quoting Homer Fink. "I am a wolf."

"No. No," Katrinka Nonningham whispered.

"They're leaving—sh-hh," Phillip Moore reminded us.

That moment I didn't care if Phillip Moore saw us or if Mr. Muncrief and Mr. Aberdenally discovered us or if the world ended with everyone frozen right where he was forever. I had my arm around Katrinka Nonningham. Life was perfect.

A loud thumping from inside one of the garbage cans interrupted us. A voice demanded, "Sell me to the man who needs a master."

"It's he. It's Homer," Katrinka exclaimed, and she was on her feet and out of my arm.

Everybody I know says, "It's him," except those girls from private schools.

14

"IF YOU WANT TO DO SOMETHING FOR ME," Homer Fink said to Katrinka, "please do not shield the light."

"You can come out now, Homer," she said. "You're safe."

Homer's knees were pressed close to his chin and his shoulders rolled forward. He blinked his eyes, and as Phillip Moore helped him to his feet he had great difficulty straightening himself.

"You look wretched," said Katrinka. "How you must have suffered." Katrinka liked that idea and she brushed Homer's hair back from his forehead.

"Move slowly. Don't take it too fast," Phillip Moore advised. "Your muscles have to get used to action again."

Homer Fink tried to raise his arms and his back was hunched. But he was smiling and seemed tremendously satisfied. "Absolutely remarkable. An incredible experience."

I explained to Homer that we had been looking for him all afternoon and I told him what had happened to Little Louie. Homer was more concerned with telling us about a Greek philosopher.

"If I hadn't remembered Diogenes I would never have thought of hiding in a barrel."

Katrinka asked if Homer wanted a drink of water, and Phillip Moore was interested in finding out if Homer had a Charley horse.

"Diogenes tried to live his life with the barest essentials," Homer went on. "That way he was able to think without distraction about the governing of men. You know it works."

"As close as you were to the school cafeteria, you should have some terrific ideas on the hot-lunch menu," I said.

"I am definitely going to recommend that every student at P.S. 79 spend an hour a week in a garbage can," Homer announced.

"I have some of my most meaningful thoughts when I'm in the bathtub," aid Katrinka.

Homer managed to straighten his back and he was moving his arms freely now. "I owe it all to you, Richard. It was you who catapulted me into the girls' yard and sent me soaring into unexplored regions of contemplation."

"I was only trying to protect you from Mr. Muncrief," I admitted. "Little Louie is in real trouble. Because of him, the boys are going to have calisthenics at recess tomorrow."

"I was hoping we would have time to go over my nominating speech this afternoon," Phillip Moore told Homer.

Homer flailed his arms and tried to run. "What we must do is create an army of young people all over the world who are willing to spend a little time in garbage cans."

"I'd take it slow introducing garbage cans into your campaign," I said.

"Are you sure the world is ready for you?" said Katrinka.

"It's not important to win every time," Homer told us.

Phillip Moore was anxious to get down to business. It was easy to see why he always made A's for homework. He started to tell Homer his ideas about the United Nations fighting poverty, but Homer no longer thought the peace organization was adequate. The experience in the barrel had inspired a new approach. Homer Fink had visions. "Students from Calcutta to Caracas, Peking to Peoria, London to Leopoldville will exile themselves in barrels to contemplate truth and justice."

Katrinka Nonningham said she thought it was the most original idea she had ever heard. "We're spoiled and that's the truth," she said. "It's time we made some sacrifices to help our fellow man."

I held fast to my clip-board. It wasn't exactly the perfect time to talk about committees and raising a campaign fund, but if there was a political situation that called for a manager, I knew this was it.

"I don't understand you, Homer," I began. "Here you have an absolutely perfect campaign issue practically forced on you and you turn it down."

Homer shook his head. "I will not take advantage of Bannerman's misfortune, Richard."

"I wouldn't expect you to," I said. "But that's not the point." I turned to Katrinka. "You're right, Katrinka. We're spoiled."

When we were on the sidewalk safely beyond the school I continued, "You're always seeing signs, Homer. How did you miss this one? He was right in front of you—bigger than life."

"Why don't you tell us what you're driving at," Katrinka said impatiently.

"Are you inferring that the divinities were

communicating and I ignored them?" asked Homer.

"Figure it out for yourself."

"Who was it, Richard? Hermes? Apollo? Zeus?"

"Mr. Aberdenally was saying some very strange things for a man who is a school custodian." I paused and then facing Homer directly I said, "I hope you weren't daydreaming in the garbage can, Homer."

I could see by Homer's expression that I had him hooked, and if I had Homer, Katrinka and Phillip were on the same line. "You were the one who taught me to look to the lowliest of creatures for divine expression."

"Are you trying to tell us Mr. Aberdenally is a divinity? Is it possible you're suggesting he's related to the man we met in the park?" Katrinka explained to Phillip about our meeting with Silenus.

As soon as Phillip was up to date I thrust my clip-board in front of me and read, "Crumbs on floor bring mouse. Mouse sign of bad luck. Who makes crumbs? Spoiled brats."

"Why are you talking like an Indian?" Katrinka asked. "Is this some kind of code between you and Homer?"

"Me savvy," said Homer Fink.

"It is a code," said Katrinka. "Homer's talking that way too."

"We only talk this way when we want to boil things down. Get to the point fast," I said. "We developed it when we were younger and Homer and I played cowboys and Indians with older boys who made us the Indians."

"How do we translate this observation into political action?" Phillip Moore wanted to know.

"In the nominating speech," I said. "Only we won't go into too much detail about how this is going to affect the starving masses of India. Let's keep it simple. Suppose we begin by recommending that no one bring more in his lunch bag than he or she can eat. Then insist that every student make an effort to clean up around his lunch area."

Phillip Moore took a notebook from his coat jacket and started to write. "Excellent point, Richard. Imagine the effects that second peanut-butter-and-jelly sandwich could have on the economy of Ruanda-Urundi?"

"Wouldn't the sandwiches be stale when they got there?" asked Katrinka.

"Phillip isn't going to suggest that we ship sandwiches," I said. "He's going to make the students aware of waste."

"It's very unlikely that Mr. Aberdenally is a god of heaven," said Homer Fink. "He must be a divinity from the underworld and I'm certain

126

it could all be conveniently explained, once we have established the identity of the mouse."

"You'll figure it out, Homer," I said. "In the meantime let's make sure we're set for the nominating assembly." Phillip seemed to feel he had the speech under control and Homer wanted to plan the demonstration. "Plan big heap pow-wow," I said to Homer before he started home. "Me walk squaw to bus."

That was all I had to say to have Katrinka Nonningham to myself.

15

SHE DIDN'T HAVE THE SLIGHEST NEED TO TALK, and as soon as Homer and Phillip were out of sight all I could do was look at Katrinka Nonningham. She held her head high. She seemed to be studying the tops of trees and passing birds and cloud formations, low in the distant sky. Rarely did she move her head. I was sure she was poised on the brink of a revelation of great beauty.

I felt lost without Homer, and I regretted having maneuvered to be with Katrinka before I had prepared wonderful things to say.

We started across Park Avenue and walked along a wing of Mount Vernon Place. There were empty benches and the stone fountain was dry. In front of us loomed the monument of George Washington. The first President stood looking south. In his hand he held his resignation as Commander in Chief. I had once written a term paper on the monument and I thought about telling Katrinka that it was the first tribute built to Washington and the money had been raised by a lottery. But even George Washington paled in the presence of Katrinka Nonningham. I couldn't speak.

When we arrived at the bus stop Katrinka moved directly to the sign and stood near the curb marked in red. She offered me her hand.

It was tan with long tapering fingers and the firm wrists I would expect from a tennis player. I was ready to say good-by when I noticed her fingernails. Katrinka Nonningham bit her fingernails, and when I knew that I said, "I'd like to see you home."

Katrinka answered, "Suit yourself."

We waited silently until the bus rolled up the hill of Charles Street, stopped, and let us board. There was a seat on the aisle near the door. Katrinka sat and offered to hold my books.

I held the hand guard near her seat. When the bus lurched forward, I rolled with the motion and didn't lose my balance. With my free hand I reached for Katrinka's shoulder and braced her so she wouldn't fall forward.

I said, "Katrinka, do you love Homer Fink?"

"I don't know what love is," she answered.

"Everybody knows something about love," I

said. "I'm sure your mother loves you and your father loves you even if he does live in California."

Katrinka blushed. "How did you know my parents were separated? Who's been talking about them?"

"You told Homer the first day we met," I said. "I was standing right there."

Katrinka lowered her eyes and studied the books on her lap.

"It'll work out. Your father will come back. You'll see."

"You have no reason to say that. Mind your own business." Katrinka thrust my books toward me and I had to let go of the hand guard.

I stood by her seat swaying with the movement of the bus. Neither of us spoke and I didn't look at her face because I didn't want our eyes to meet. Girls certainly were different from boys. And in a lot more ways than anyone could discover by looking over the fence into their yard.

Most of the people got off when the bus stopped at North Avenue and the seat next to Katrinka was empty. She moved to the window and I sat beside her.

"My cousin goes to private school," I said. "She's great in field hockey. Do you play?"

Katrinka Nonningham said, "No."

"That's right—you like individual sports like

tennis," I said. "And I'll bet you're great in skiing. Do you like to ski?"

Katrinka's voice was softer when she answered, "Yes."

"Look, Katrinka, Homer Fink is my best friend and if you like him so much and you want to consider him your one and only boy friend, that's great. I'm not trying to come between you and Homer."

"I know that," Katrinka answered.

The bus passed Homewood and Katrinka was looking out at the green lawns and the buildings of the Johns Hopkins University. "It's better that my father lives in California. He and Mommie used to fight all the time. They screamed and threw things." Then she said, "He's been gone exactly one year tomorrow."

"I had a friend at camp whose parents were divorced," I told her. "His name was Archie Carrister. Only Archie's father used to take him to Denver, Colorado, every summer. The judge made Archie go there. He didn't like it at first. But now he says it's just great. He learned to ride a horse and other things in Denver, and he always gets great grades for geography reports because he knows all about Denver."

"I'm not ever going to go to California. Nobody in the world will ever make me visit there," said Katrinka. "I never want to see my father again in my life."

"Archie said things like that. But after a while he changed his mind."

Katrinka reeled around to face me. Her eyes were opened wide and her blonde hair whipped across her face. "Keep quiet, Richard. You don't know the least thing about what you're saying."

She turned back to the window and I waited a while before I asked, "Do you have a brother or sister?"

Katrinka shook her head—meaning no.

"Well, if you don't get angry all the time, I could be your friend."

At Katrinka's stop I got off the bus and walked beside her. She seemed to take it for granted that I would escort her home. We left Charles Street and started up a block called Howard's Lane. There were three houses on the street. Each had a lawn and trees and hedges separating it from the street.

"That's where I live," Katrinka said as we passed a house of red brick with white shutters and two marble pillars on the porch. There was a driveway leading up to it and I had the feeling it was a mansion.

"If you're not in too much of a hurry to get home, we could walk for a minute," said Katrinka.

I said, "It's no trouble at all. My favorite aunt lives near here. She just moved and she's always asking me to visit her. Her name is Jennie Rothman. It's in the phone book, listed under my cousin Bruce. He can drive me home."

There was a light wind and it swept her hair, whipping strands across her face. Katrinka's eyes were half-closed, and the look I had thought could see right through people was no longer there. We continued around the block and I heard Katrinka say, "When Homer Fink called me the evening after we'd met in the park, I didn't want to talk to him. I hung up twice. I had made up my mind never to talk to any boys again ever—they just lie to me."

"Homer Fink never lies," I said. "He wouldn't have called you Aphrodite if he didn't believe it."

That made her smile. "Wouldn't it be sad to be the goddess of love and not understand the first thing about it." And then Katrinka said, "Oh, it would be so wonderful to be Aphrodite, Richard. Promise—swear never to tell Homer Fink that I'm not."

I wasn't sure what she meant, but I had the feeling it had something to do with her father leaving.

Katrinka's hands were resting on the gate and her hair was all over her face and my arms were filled with books.

"I promise," I said, and I leaned forward and kissed Katrinka Nonningham's lips.

"See you tomorrow." I ran to my aunt's.

16

Brian Spitzer made the nominating speech for little Louie Bannerman.

Because he was in our class, I had counted on Brian's support. But Brian Spitzer would never give up a chance to have the stage. It was clever of Louie to ask Brian to represent him. Not only had he picked up valuable support in our homeroom, but Louie could be sure Brian would say exactly what he was told without arguing about his own ideas.

"The Bannerman platform is a medical approach to the ills of P.S. 79," Brian announced. "He has diagnosed our ailments and prescribed remedies." I wondered if the other students were aware that Louie Bannerman's father was a doctor and that Louis planned to go to medical school. The speech didn't sound like anything Brian Spitzer would write.

Brian explained that if elected Louie would offer a plan to relieve the noise in the cafeteria. There was applause and I sat on the edge of the seat, fearful that the Bannerman platform would include a peanut-butter sandwich in every foreign-aid package.

"Bannerman will prescribe a program for supervised play in the yard after school," continued Brian. I was relieved that the cafeteria program was complete. On my clip-board I made a note to question Bannerman on recess calisthenics.

"Louie has diagnosed our need for a school prom," said Brian. "And he is creating a formula to achieve it."

The girls shrieked and Little Louie stood on his seat and blew them kisses. I remembered the night of Elaine Steigmar's party when Little Louie watched television with Elaine's parents all through spin the bottle.

Politics can change people's personalities even faster than Homer's mythology, I thought to myself.

The success of Brian's speech was capped by the Bannerman demonstration. Marvin Bloom marched in beating an old drum and Jerry Trout followed, blowing call-to-arms on the bugle.

On the stage Miss Everswell whispered to Mr. Muncrief, and the assistant principal hurried to close the windows overlooking the neighboring Sixth Regiment Armory.

Bannerman's supporters in the seventh grade led the procession. They chanted:

> Bannerman—Bannerman,
> He's our man.
> If he can't do it,
> Nobody can.

They didn't seem the least aware that they were borrowing a City High School football cheer. Right behind the seventh-graders marched a dozen students from the eighth. They carried a large cone made out of cardboard. It was supposed to be a rocket. Somebody had worn out a great many magic markers writing: AIR OR SEA OR LAND—VOTE FOR BANNERMAN.

As the demonstrators started up the center aisle they filled the air with paper airplanes bearing messages encouraging the election of Little Louie.

Again Miss Everswell whispered to Mr. Muncrief. I suppose they were making plans for cleaning up the auditorium.

The ninth-grade delegation brought up the rear. Carrying the sign from the schoolyard, they chanted:

Fink—Phooey,
Vote for Louie.

I was beginning to feel less certain about leaving the plans for our demonstration to Homer, but because I was in the audience I would be able to organize a "spontaneous" demonstration from the floor. Patty Esposito and two girls from her class were prepared to swoon when Homer made his grand entrance.

The Bannerman demonstrators circled the auditorium twice. The students were seated, and Miss Everswell introduced Phillip Moore.

Phillip was wearing a tweed jacket and black knit tie. His hair was slicked back and the expression on his face made me feel he was ready to address a joint session of Congress and deliver the State of the Union message—nothing less than that. If we were looking for the most popular boy in school to present Homer's nominating speech, the response to Phillip Moore left no doubt as to how right we were.

Phillip raised a hand signaling for silence, but the audience was on its feet screaming, "We want Moore. We want Moore." There didn't seem to be a single boy or girl in the auditorium—including the demonstrators for Bannerman and Fink—who didn't cheer Phillip. The boys carrying Little Louie's sign were hollering, "Score with Moore," and we had trouble in our ranks when the girls who were supposed to close their eyes and faint for Homer forgot their cue and collapsed in honor of Phillip.

"Some of my friends have been kind enough to ask why I didn't make myself available for the presidency of the school," Phillip Moore began. "The reason is—Homer Fink can do more for the world."

There was a restless stirring in the crowd and I heard a voice behind me whisper, "Let's draft him." A scattering of hands was raised from the front of the room and I had visions of a nomination from the floor. I looked at Phillip Moore standing on the stage of the school auditorium. He looked so cool—so all-around—so perfect. He was the boy all our parents wanted us to be—the kind of student of which every teacher is most proud. I had a wavering doubt—were we wrong to support Homer Fink when Phillip Moore was available? I thought of Homer and the way he had won his reputation as the funniest boy in school. I remembered Homer daydreaming—inhabiting a private world removed from the classrooms of P.S. 79. Homer spoke of truth and justice and I was wondering if it was true or just to have enlisted Phillip Moore, the natural leader of our school, to work for Homer.

But then I remembered my father saying,

"So Homer Fink is your man." And the answer seemed to be—Homer was my man. Homer felt "called" and he claimed to have seen "signs," but when the chips were down and the decision had to be made, Homer Fink had dared. I was thinking that sooner or later Phillip Moore would be standing on a platform somewhere and that he would probably be accepting a great responsibility and setting everybody straight on what to do about sending grain to Asia or balancing the budget. But this was Homer's time. He made us all feel young and alive —even Katrinka Nonningham, who was the most beautiful girl in the world, but felt unloved because her father lived in California.

I wasn't going to let Homer stand outside the auditorium door and wait forever.

From my seat in the center of the hall I stood and called, "Fink. Fink. Fink." A chorus of voices joined me. The hands went down from the front of the room and Mr. Muncrief had to quiet the audience to get on with the speeches.

Phillip Moore told them all about the sandwich proposal and he discussed "youth's responsibility to a growing world crisis," but very few students were listening. Most of us were thinking about Homer Fink and remembering how daring he could be and wondering what he had dreamed up for his demonstration.

17

THE DOORS TO THE ASSEMBLY HALL were opened. There was the noise of rustling skirts and anxious voices and then silence. A teacher in the back of the room instructed the students to stay in their seats and a seventh-grader was informed he could "get a drink of water later."

We heard a dog bark and then the loud broken blast of a horn. It was a sound that could not have come from a clarinet, trombone, or a bugle.

Again the sound of the horn filled the auditorium and the march for Homer Fink began. A man in knee-length suspended pants and a

Tyrolean hat entered. A ram's horn was slung over his shoulder and he held a staff. I recognized him as the shepherd we had seen in the park.

Students gasped and giggled and several girls clapped their hands. A thin, ruddy-faced man with long hair, the shepherd stood for a moment as if paralyzed by the presence of so many children. Homer Fink called to the shepherd in Greek and the next thing we saw was a sheep running down the aisle.

A small sign made of cardboard shirt backings was slung over Argus' back. On one side it read: εὐλαβεῖσθαι τὴν κύνα. The other flank carried the translation: BEWARE THE DOG—Aristophanes.

The shepherd dashed to catch the dog who was chasing the sheep, and the students of P.S. 79 cheered. I stood on top of my seat. It was against the school's rules, but no one seemed to remember the rules any more. The teachers who weren't stunned were enjoying the Homer Fink demonstration as much as the students. On the stage Miss Everswell and Mr. Muncrief shook their heads as if to say: "It looks real, but it just can't be."

Flute players from the school orchestra were next. They wore togas and sandals and the girls had garlands of flowers in their hair. Then came two boys from the school newspaper carry-

ing tablets covered with bond paper to re-
semble parchment. In the midst of the procession was the old man Homer had told us was
Silenus. He towered over the student demonstrators. Staggering down the aisle as he drank
from a Pepsi-Cola bottle, the old man stopped
along his route to distribute soft drinks in paper
cups.

The parading ninth-graders were costumed
in togas too. Sheets, cut to form semicircles,
were worn with the straight sides up, one end
extended over the left shoulder reaching nearly
to the ground. Even though he couldn't tie a
bowknot for his shoelaces, Homer Fink had
managed to teach a half-dozen students to make
and wear a perfect toga.

Elaine Steigmar looked so sensational in her
Greek robes that several of the ninth-grade
boys applauded, and Brian Spitzer forgot all
about his speech for Louie Bannerman and
whistled. Cradling a straw basket, Elaine scat-
tered flowers in her path. She was preparing the
assembly for the guest of honor.

A loud clang echoed from beyond the auditorium and the demonstrators halted. All eyes
turned to the door. The time was right for
Homer Fink, the candidate, to enter. I wondered if he would appear as Zeus riding his
thunder car or Julius Caesar, uncrowned king
of Rome.

But it wasn't Homer who capped the great parade. My brother Pete waddled through the doors. There was a saucepan in one hand, a coffee pot in the other.

Pete managed three steps, slammed the pots together, and announced, "*Amo. Amas. Amat.*" He was down. He was up. Two steps forward and anxious hands stretched from the crowd to support him.

Another Latin student coached him. "*Amamus. Amatis. Amant.*" However, Homer Fink wasn't signaling for the conjugation of the verb "to love."

"Aphrodite," said Homer, and Katrinka Nonningham entered.

Taking Pete by the hand, she started around the auditorium. Homer wanted Katrinka to represent Aphrodite, the goddess of love, and I don't think there was a boy or girl in the auditorium who would have given him an argument, even if they knew she went to Park School.

Katrinka wore a toga and golden sandals and there was a crown in her hair. When I looked at her she reminded me of the day we had met. I thought of sailboats again. I could see Katrinka, dressed exactly the way she was, standing on the windward washboard of a racing boat—eyes wide and bold and staring right into the sun in a brilliant blue world. I wanted

143

to go to her and kiss her again, but when she passed she seemed to look right through me, as if Homer Fink and she were linked by a destiny none of us mortals would ever completely understand.

The attending maidens filled the air with flowers and the shepherd sounded his ram's horn. The flute players piped a tune and Argus barked.

After the last of the demonstrators abandoned the hall, we started back to our classrooms. I heard a seventh-grader say, "I'm taking Latin next semester even if French is more practical."

"It's not that I have anything against Plato," a serious ninth-grader commented. "It's just that I've never read him."

Even Marvin Bloom admitted, "I dig those crazy togas."

I was wondering if Greek and Latin would help me to understand girls.

18

THERE WASN'T MUCH INFORMATION available on Pan and Silenus or what arrangement Katrinka Nonningham had made to skip school. I was particularly anxious to find out how Homer had convinced my mother to let Pete attend the assembly. But there was little time for going over old news during lunch hour.

Mr. Muncrief met us in the cafeteria. Dressed in a gray sweat suit and sneakers, he announced that there would be calisthenics after lunch in the boy's yard.

Then Little Louie Bannerman appeared at our table. He was wearing gym shorts and sneakers. "Be fit and survive," said Little Louie. "Join the Bannerman physical-education program."

As he trotted to the next table, shaking hands, smiling, and waving, I heard Louie confide to a seventh-grader, "Keep your eyes on me. I'll be up front."

I told Homer, "We had better talk to Mr. Muncrief about making you a demonstrator, too."

Homer Fink said, "I'd rather read a book."

"I'm sure you would," I said. "But you made a great impression at the assembly this morning, so let's keep the band wagon rolling." I threw away my napkin and sandwich wrap and started after Mr. Muncrief.

"May I remind you Louis Bannerman enjoys exercise," said Homer. "He even likes rope-climbing."

"We can't let Little Louie have all this exposure without fighting for equal time," I advised my candidate.

"There's nothing in Machiavelli about equal time," said Homer.

"Machiavelli didn't have a television set," I answered. "Besides, politics is my hobby and you can take my word for it."

"I'm certainly lucky to have you on my side," sighed Homer.

Mr. Muncrief fastened the top button of Homer's shirt. "Where's your note for absence from school yesterday afternoon? The rules state specifically all absence and lateness must be explained by a written note from home."

Homer placed one hand over his heart and raised the other. "Πάντα νομιστί," he said. "All things by law."

"Precisely," said Mr. Muncrief. "And that sheep and that dog and the little boy who should have been in nursery school. What were they doing in the auditorium this morning? I would certainly like to know the meaning of that."

"Pete is Richard's brother," said Homer Fink. "He loves a parade." Homer started to quote again in Greek, but Mr. Muncrief interrupted him.

"I'll see you this afternoon at three-thirty in my office. In the meantime . . ." Mr. Muncrief noticed the collar of Homer's jacket was back on his shoulders. As he adjusted it, Mr. Muncrief said softly, "We're going to have to take a little more care with our appearance now that we're in the public eye."

It was a perfect opening for me to explain that Homer would like to join Little Louie as a demonstrator.

"I had no idea you were athletically inclined," the assistant principal said to Homer. "Indeed I would prefer to have you right up front where I can keep my eye on you. We'll put a little beef and muscle on you yet, Homer," he added.

As we started to the yard I suggested Homer put on his sweat suit. Homer Fink told me that changing clothes was one of the rare things in the world he considered a bore.

We lined up with an arm interval between each student. At the far end of the yard, Mr. Muncrief stood on a raised platform flanked by Little Louie and Homer. Both candidates were on the ground with their hands and feet braced beneath them to power their rise.

"One," commanded Mr. Muncrief, and Homer and Louie began their demonstration of a push-up.

"Back straight," we heard Mr. Muncrief remind them. "Push up. Heave."

Little Louie completed the first step with ease. From his upright position he gazed at Homer Fink who remained on the ground.

Mr. Muncrief said, "The idea is to exercise your arms and leg muscles by pushing up, Homer."

Homer maneuvered his hands and readjusted his feet and at last with a great push managed to raise his chest by arching his back.

Mr. Muncrief dropped to his knees and made an effort to set Homer's body; he put Little Louie in charge of leading the rest of us.

"Up. Down. One. Two," Louie repeated.

"Lay off. Slow down," Jerry Trout demanded.

Brian Spitzer called, "You're breaking my back."

Most of us dropped out after the twelfth push-up, but Phillip Moore had no difficulty keeping pace with Little Louie.

"Hold your position," Mr. Muncrief directed Homer.

With a tremendous effort Homer shoved up. His shirttail overlapped his belt and I noticed Homer's feet were out of his unlaced shoes. His long red hair fell across his eyes, but there was a big smile on Homer's face.

"That's it. Fine," said Mr. Muncrief. "Now try without my support."

Homer Fink slowly lowered his body.

With the exception of the boys who were interested in the endurance contest between Little Louie and Phillip Moore, the rest of us followed Homer's progress.

"Steady. Steady." Mr. Muncrief encouraged him. "You can do it. I know you can do it, Homer."

Homer's arms trembled and there was a thin line of sweat rolling down his cheek. "*Tendit in ardua virtus.* Courage exerts itself in difficulties. Ovid," Homer reminded himself.

"Give up?" Little Louie called to Phillip Moore. "Are you worn out?"

Phillip replied, "I'm fine."

"Gently now," Mr. Muncrief told Homer. "Not your chest! Touch your chin to the ground and you'll have it."

Homer's elbows were pressed to the side and his cuffs hung to his knuckles. Biting his lip, he lowered another inch. "Bear up. τέτλαθι—Homer groaned. "*Iliad*, Book I."

"Sink, Fink, sink," a voice urged from the rear of the yard. Homer's legs quivered and his body shook, but he made another inch of painful progress.

"Don't give up," Mr. Muncrief pleaded. "One push-up—only one." And then the assistant principal said, " τέτλαθι —"

With the word from the *Iliad* ringing in our ears, we saw Homer stretch his neck. The muscles strained and Homer resembled a turtle rising from his shell. He came closer and closer until at last the tip of Homer Fink's chin was a fraction of an inch from the ground.

Suddenly Mr. Muncrief slapped his hand against the platform and proclaimed, "He made it."

Students rushed forward hollering versions of the Greek word that inspired the victory. They slapped Homer's back and pumped his hand and treated Homer Fink as if he had hit a home run in the last of the ninth with bases loaded or broken the tape to win the Olympic marathon.

19

"COUNT ME IN," Brian Spitzer told me after school that day. "My arms are still sore from all those push-ups. Who wants Little Louie for president of the school anyway? Homer is more laughs."

I was waiting for Homer to return from Mr. Muncrief's office. It had been almost an hour since the last class and I was beginning to face the fact that my candidate had detention. I wasn't particularly happy to have Brian on our side again, but as a random sample it indicated the polls were in our favor.

Homer Fink was smiling as he started down the steps from P.S. 79. He swung his bookbag high in the air, tried to catch it, and missed.

Making two big circles with his thunbs and fore-
fingers he exclaimed. "I've solved it. He's Apollo."

I said, "Pick up your schoolbag and I'll treat
you to an ice cream soda, Homer."

"As you so perceptibly observed the other
day, Richard, Mr. Muncrief is something special."

I picked up Homer's bookbag, and he followed me up the street. "Do you have to bring
a note from home to explain your absence?
Did Mr. Muncrief lay it on because of the sheep
and Argus and all the ringers you brought to
school for your demonstration?"

Homer pounded me on the back. "Remember
your Shelley?" He recited:

All men who do or even imagine ill
   Fly me, and from the glory of my ray
Good minds and open actions take new might.

"Isn't that Mr. Muncrief all over?"

I said, "If you're planning to put that to music for a campaign song, Homer, forget it. I'd
suggest you start thinking along the lines of
'Buckle Down, Winsockie.'" Then I said,
"What's going on in detention anyway? Your
imagination is running away with you."

"It wasn't my imagination that brought the
mouse to Mr. Muncrief's office," said Homer. "It
was no vision of mine when he opened the window and greeted her."

"You don't mean to tell me Mr. Muncrief is hiding the mouse, the one Mr. Aberdenally is running all over the school trying to kill?"

"Exactly," said Homer. "The spirit of Apollo Smintheus is upon him."

"I definitely need a soda." I thrust Homer's schoolbag at him and he took it.

"We call her Persephone," said Homer Fink, and on the way to the soda fountain he told me the story of the queen of Hades who spent half her time on earth and the rest in the underworld. But I was thinking Persephone could prove a valuable bit of information if Mr. Muncrief became impatient with Homer during the campaign.

Because the owner spent lots of time decorating the window with displays of the history of drugs, Goldenheimer's Drugstore on North and Park was Homer's favorite. The window was devoted to penicillin that month and there were pictures and samples of roots and cards explaining things such as "Antibiosis was first used by P. Vuillemin in 1889."

Goldenheimer's was different from the chain store up the street. It wasn't only the windows. We would have to look for about ten minutes if we wanted to find a comic in Goldenheimer's and then it would always be a funny book and not a war story. Mr. Goldenheimer had very definite ideas about magazines and comic books. Not that we could tell from talking to him. He had very little to say.

When Homer and I arrived, Mr. Goldenheimer was in the back making a prescription. A customer was sitting at the counter drinking a cup of coffee. Mrs. Goldenheimer had set his place with a paper doily and a napkin and a glass of water.

I ordered a chocolate soda with vanilla ice cream, but Homer wanted to see a menu.

Mrs. Goldenheimer seemed pleased by this request. She made the menus, running them off on a mimeograph machine that was in the rear of the store. There was always soup and sandwich and a dessert of the day. That was called the "special luncheon" and it was featured for 99 cents. The Goldenheimers must have done a great lunch business or received lots of orders on the telephone because the place was never crowded in the afternoon. It was hard to figure out how they could afford to keep changing the menus and re-doing the windows and setting every place with a clean doily without going bankrupt.

We didn't order the luncheon, but Homer Fink was interested in the dessert that went with the special. He was the only boy I knew who would stop for an after-school snack and order rice pudding.

Mrs. Goldenheimer handed Homer the menu. "The tapioca is very tasty," she said. "Made it myself fresh, today."

"Ah—tapioca," Homer repeated. "I can't resist."

Mrs. Goldenheimer smiled again and wiped the counter in front of Homer's place, even though it was already sparkling clean. "One chocolate soda with vanilla ice and one tapioca —working!"

"Tapioca," Homer said again.

"Tapioca," said Mrs. Goldenheimer.

Homer Fink snapped his fingers. "Tapioca, Cha. Cha. Cha."

After we were served, Mrs. Goldenheimer disappeared into the back of the store where her husband was filling a prescription. We could hear her telling him. "Tapioca. Cha. Cha. Cha."

"Not when I'm working, please," was Mr. Goldenheimer's response. I just knew he was making the most accurate and sanitary prescription in the world.

Homer was eating his tapioca and I was sipping my soda when two boys from the Latin School entered the store. One had on a gray wool sweater beneath his sports coat and the other was wearing a tan poplin raincoat. The raincoat was old and dirty, but on the fellow from the Latin School it seemed neat, the perfect coat to be wearing on a fall day when weaker fellows would be wearing overcoats.

They nodded in the direction of Homer and whispered.

Homer waved a spoonful of tapioca. "It's good the spirit of Apollo has entered Mr. Muncrief, and fortunate, too, that he has Persephone for company."

I tried to change the subject, but Homer went on discussing the loneliness of the life of an assistant principal.

The fellows from the Latin School sat at the fountain and the boy in the poplin raincoat said, "Pardon me, but isn't *he* Homer Fink?"

We introduced ourselves and Oliver, the boy in the wool sweater, asked how Homer's campaign was going. He wanted to know if the students at 79 were "thinking with Fink."

Homer was ready to launch into a thought project at once, but I was interested in where they had learned about Homer's campaign.

Oliver told us that their schoolmates who had heard Homer speak at the B. and O. terminal had spread the word.

Wally, the boy in the poplin raincoat, told us, " 'Think with Fink' is always scrawled on blackboards, and yesterday it was written in chalk on the north grounds."

Oliver said, "The question in our forum this quarter is—Is there really a Homer Fink?"

I was about to ask how they recognized Homer when Oliver asked what Homer was eating.

Homer said something about "a farinaceous food substance prepared from cassava starch." That was exactly the way the fellows from Boys Latin placed their order. Mrs. Goldenheimer was bewildered until Homer said, "Cha. Cha. Cha." Then Mrs. Goldenheimer prepared two more plates of tapioca.

I was mushing the last of my ice cream with the chocolate syrup at the bottom of my soda when Oliver asked if we were on Lafayette's soccer team. I guess all public schools have names as well as numbers but I never thought of myself as going to Lafayette until our meeting with Oliver and Wally. Except in our school song, we just about never called our school "Lafayette."

Homer told them we didn't have a soccer team, but we were making great progress with push-ups.

Oliver thought that was funny and Wally said Homer Fink certainly lived up to his reputation.

"We don't have a varsity in any sport," I told them. "The only time we compete against other schools is in the city-wide track meet."

"Layfayette will be playing us in soccer," said Wally. "And that's for sure!"

"We're inviting your ninth-grade boys to lunch and scrimmage with us on Friday," Oliver continued, "Our varsity committee had a meeting this afternoon with a fellow from your school."

I crunched my straws. "The boy who spoke to you—was his name Bannerman?"

Oliver looked at Wally, and Wally shrugged his shoulders. They couldn't remember the name.

"Was he kind of thin and wearing glasses? Very neat and always taking notes as if he were writing prescriptions?"

Wally said that was an accurate description, and Oliver remembered that the fellow had been very careful to shake everyone's hand.

"It's Little Louie," I told Homer. "Bannerman has scored a political coup."

Homer wasn't the least distressed. "After all these years of student clamor for a varsity team, Little Louie had come to grips with the problem and resolved it." He raised his tapioca dish. "Here's to Little Louie."

Oliver and Wally joined Homer's toast, hesitating only to see if Homer intended to drink from the tapioca dish. (He didn't.) I tried to keep my chocolate syrup going with a shot of free soda.

The campaign had taken a sudden turn for the worse, and it was no help having my candidate so enthusiastic about the opposition.

20

"I DIDN'T KNOW UNTIL TODAY there was a shepherd in Druid Hill Park," my mother told my father at dinner that night. "A very pleasant man he is too. Pete was delighted with him."

"*Amo*," said Pete and he slapped his spoon against the table of his baby tender.

"This is the first I've heard of a shepherd in Baltimore City," said my father. "Did you discover him?"

My mother explained that the shepherd was a friend of Homer Fink's and then she said to me, "Who was that beautiful young lady who brought Pete home from the assembly?"

"That's Katrinka," I said. "She goes to Park School and she's heading up the women's division of the Fink campaign."

My mother handed Romulus a teething ring and gave Remus a rattle.

"Beautiful girls and kissing babies are traditional in politics," my father said as he handed Pete a rubber cup in exchange for his spoon. "But how about the shepherd? Is Homer appealing to the rural vote?"

"Homer doesn't exactly think he's a shepherd. More or less he's convinced the man is Pan."

"Have some Brussels sprouts," my mother said to me. "You must learn to eat vegetables, Richard. I don't want you filling up on bread and potatoes."

"Pan who?" asked my father.

"Pan, the Greek god of nature." I took two Brussels sprouts and put them on my plate.

My father said, "It's just a game, of course. Homer's father is a classics professor and I suppose it's to be expected."

"Homer thinks the old drunk who wanders around the park is Silenus." I pushed the Brussels sprouts into the far corner of my plate.

Romulus dropped his teething ring and screamed. My mother picked it up and then Remus threw his rattle to the floor. When my mother handed it back to him, Romulus let go of his teething ring again.

"Homer's been telling me Katrinka is Aphrodite and he's just about convinced himself beyond a question of doubt that Mr. Muncrief is Apollo."

"Mr. Muncrief, the assistant principal of the school?" said my father.

"It's so refreshing to hear a young person speak with admiration of a teacher," said my mother. She retrieved the teething ring and then went after the rattle. The twins were gurgling and smiling and having a ball.

"Homer thinks all the children in the world should spend a few hours a day curled up in a garbage can—thinking."

My father said, "I can see that your candidate is keeping you busy."

"I wouldn't worry about Homer," said my mother. "Some people just pass from childhood into adolescence more slowly than others. I'm sure it's a game and Homer is having fun playing it."

"How's it going over with the electorate?" asked my father.

"The kids at school think Homer's a riot."

"*Omni—Omni—*," screamed Pete and he threw the rubber cup across the room.

"As long as Homer Fink knows the difference between the truth and the games he's playing I suppose he'll be all right." Then my father

161

said, "What do you think, Richard? Are you beginning to have visions of Greek deities too?"

"Only one and sometimes I have my doubts about her." I sliced a sprout.

"Homer is campaigning for a return to the classics," announced my mother. "It runs in his family. It's just as simple as that."

Pete climbed to the table of his tender and reached over to my plate. He was always trying to filch my food. Usually I stopped him but this time he was headed for half of a Brussels sprout.

"Now Peter, don't bother Richard when he's eating." Mother was on her way under the table to recover Remus's teething ring.

"It's O.K.," I said. "He's my brother. I don't mind sharing."

"Sooner or later Homer will have to face the fact that there are no gods on earth—only people," said my father. "And that's a truth that's been the last straw for more than one reformer."

"Homer's never really discouraged by people," I said. "If anything, he's the first one to find things unusual or exciting about them. The way things are going now, I wouldn't be surprised if Homer votes for Louie Bannerman."

My mother thought that was wonderful and even my father had to admit it was a new twist. I concentrated on watching Pete stuff a Brussels sprout into his mouth.

"At your age children change every day," said my mother.

"Me more. Me more," Pete said in the direction of my remaining sprout.

"I don't think James Farley and Mark Hanna combined could manage your Homer Fink," said my father.

"Don't take Homer too seriously," advised my mother. Just thinking about Homer made my mother smile. She collected the teething ring and rattle and tied them to a string on the baby tenders.

"*Amo*," Pete said with his mouth full.

"We love you too," said my father. He squeezed my shoulder and I said, "I sure hope Homer Fink can learn to play soccer from a book."

21

ACCORDING TO MR. MUNCRIEF we were visiting the Latin School to put napkins on our laps. The assistant principal gathered the ninth-graders in the assembly hall on Thursday and spoke to us. He spent about twenty minutes diagraming a "place setting."

It seems the last time the boys of P.S. 79 were invited to the Latin School for lunch was in 1942. There had been a discussion about whether the hosts were serving butter or oleomargarine and the representatives of P.S. 79 resolved it by flipping portions against the walls. Butter would stick, according to the theory, oleo wouldn't. Latin's dietitian also made the error of serving fresh peas. Solemnly Mr. Muncrief told us that our boys used the peas as "projectiles."

Before returning to the more serious business of "discipline and manners," Mr. Muncrief had a few words about the soccer game. He quoted Grantland Rice, who believed it didn't matter who won or lost as long as you played the game fair and square. That was the assistant principal's way of letting us know he expected us to lose. Homer thought Mr. Muncrief was inspired by Apollo, but most of us would have been happier if he had diagramed soccer strategy rather than table manners.

"Remember now—knife blade always faces in," said Mr. Muncrief. "And we help ourselves to pie à la mode with a fork."

Brian Spitzer wanted to know if we were having apple pie or blueberry. Mr. Muncrief told him he did not know the menu but wanted us to be prepared for every emergency.

After reminding us about saying "please" and "thank you" and pointing out the spoons and forks to use for soup, entrees, and salads, the assistant principal erased the blackboard. Then, he told us, "Above all else, do *not* be critical of the food. Try your best to eat what is on your plate. And for no reason whatsoever express dislike for what is served." Mr. Muncrief must have remembered some of the expressions he had seen in the cafeteria when Alma Melchere was trying to trade her sardine sandwich at the boys' table for a peanut butter and jelly.

Elaine Steigmar wanted to know if the girls had been asked to lunch too. When Mr. Muncrief told her the girls had only been invited to see the game, there was a long sigh of disappointment. I guess public school girls really dig those poplin raincoats.

Then Elaine suggested we organize a girls' cheering section. Her sister was a cheerleader at Forest Park High and Elaine promised to bring her megaphone. Mr. Muncrief agreed but warned us not to be rowdy.

During most of the meeting Trudy Deal had her hand up. I don't think she knew exactly what she wanted to say until she was called upon, but Trudy didn't like to take chances with being ignored. She was popping out of her seat and ohing and ahing as if the gym were on fire and we'd all be suffocated in seconds if she didn't get the floor. It was Trudy's idea that the girls turn out for the game wearing their togas. "You know Homer Fink is so interested in the Greeks and all, and them being the Latin School."

"They being," said Mr. Muncrief.

It took several seconds for Trudy to realize Mr. Muncrief was correcting her grammar. By that time all the girls were squealing about wearing togas and Mr. Muncrief could not hear Louie Bannerman when he said, "P.S. 79 should conduct a nonpartisan interschool policy."

"That's a break for us," I told Homer on our way from the auditorium. "Little Louie may be captain of the team, but we'll have the best of the cheering section."

Homer kicked one foot and then the other. "Ball control. Trapping. Tackling. Heading." He bobbed his head as if he had on a tight collar.

I said, "I suppose you've been reading a book on soccer."

Homer Fink's answer was, "Soccer was introduced into England by the Romans. Beware of Latin booters." I also learned that soccer is played in more countries and seen by more people than any other sport in the world. You sure couldn't have proved it at the 79 practice session that afternoon.

Little Louie called for all the boys who were interested in the team to meet at Druid Hill Park. It was no help to Homer's campaign to have Louie Bannerman running things, but I forced myself to put principle over personality and listened to Little Louie. "Soccer is played with eleven-man teams. There is a goalie, a right fullback, a left fullback—"

"Just like football," Marvin Bloom interrupted. "Let's play."

Little Louie tried to explain that there was a great difference between the two games but when Marvin heard about the center, right, and left halfback, Little Louie's warning was wasted.

167

Jerry Trout was impressed with the fact that there was a center forward. Jerry is just about the best basketball player at P.S. 79 (with the exception of Phillip Moore, who is the best in everything) and was sure he could play soccer.

Little Louie explained the other positions—right and left wings and right and left insides, but as far as the boys of P.S. 79 were concerned you kicked the ball toward the goal and that was all there was to soccer.

Dividing us into two teams, Little Louie took charge of one group and asked Phillip Moore to run the other. Homer and I were on Phillip's squad and for all Little Louie's insistence upon a nonpartisan varsity the scrimmage definitely seemed political.

Several seconds after the kickoff from center, Brian Spitzer crashed into Homer and sent him sprawling. Homer stood up, smiled, and announced, "Charging from behind is prohibited in accordance with the rule established in 1870."

No one was going to argue with that.

Several minutes later, Homer explained to Jerry Trout that when the ball was in play only the goalie was allowed to use his hands. "That condition became effective in 1871."

The scrimmage wasn't turning out to be much more than a kicking contest. One side would boot the ball up the field and the other would kick it back. There was very little dribbling and practically no passing during the practice.

Homer Fink kept advising. "Use your head. Use your head."

Most of us were convinced that came from Plato, too, and we expected Homer to quote the original Greek. But when Phillip Moore deflected the ball with his forehead, we got the idea.

Little Louie finally brought the ball up the field by himself. He had a tricky way of dribbling with the inside of his foot and when another boy tried to boot the ball away from him Little Louie stopped the ball dead in its tracks by stepping on it and holding it with the sole of his foot. Neil Machen was playing the goal for us, and from the way he was shifting around and waving his hands he seemed to think he was on ice skates holding a hockey stick. Anyway, Little Louie passed Neil with a fast boot.

That was the lone score of the afternoon. Little Louie spent the rest of the time lining up a first team. He put Phillip Moore at goal and suggested that Homer Fink play right fullback. "You seem to know the rules, Homer," said Louie Bannerman. "And we need someone who understands the game on our first team."

I became suspicious of Little Louie's lineup when Brian Spitzer said, "It would be just like Homer Fink to cost us this game and if he does—I'll positively vote for Bannerman."

22

"WHAT HAPPENED to truth and justice and contemplating the governing of men from a garbage can?" Phillip Moore asked Homer Fink in school the next morning.

"I was kind of wondering why we haven't been seeing the head of our women's committee around lately," I said.

Homer told us, "*Maxima enim est hominum semper patientia virtus.*"

Before he could translate, an eighth-grade boy who overheard him said, "I wouldn't be quoting the enemy on the day of the big game if I were you, Homer Fink."

"The greatest of human virtues is always patience," Homer announced cheerfully.

We were standing in the hall between classes and I told Homer, "You better lay low with the Latin and stick with the Greek for a while. That kid does have a point."

At one o'clock we had a farewell rally. Little Louie took advantage of his position as head of the team to say a few words. He promised we would all do our best to make our school proud. "I feel honored to have contributed in some small way to establishing this contact," Little Louie concluded. "And I know the rest of the team is not going to let you down."

It was corny for Louie to put on that modest act about "contributing in some small way," but Mrs. Everswell, the principal, ate it up. When she complimented us for "initiative" everyone knew exactly about whom she was talking. Little Louie Bannerman received a big cheer. With less than a week to go before the election, it wasn't encouraging to the Fink campaign.

Oliver and Wally, the boys we had met at Goldenheimer's Drugstore, were on the welcoming committee. Little Louie accepted their greeting, but they addressed themselves to Homer Fink. "Tapioca. Tapioca. Cha. Cha. Cha."

"Is that some kind of password?" Little Louie wanted to know. I told him it was a Latin song Homer Fink had written.

Oliver and Wally led us into the dining room and directed us to a long wooden table. The

Latin School boys ate in a great hall with a high ceiling. There were plaques on the walls with the names of honor students and championship teams.

A group of faculty stood by the head table. We arranged our places with a boy from the host school between each of the Lafayette players. (They kept calling our school "Lafayette," and that's what we were for the rest of the afternoon.)

The dining room quieted when a man in a vested tweed suit rang a bell.

Except for Marvin Bloom, we had the idea that something had to be said or done before it was right to sit down and begin eating. Marvin plunged into his seat, put two rolls on his plate, and made for the butter.

"We say Grace before partaking," a man whom the Latin boys called a "master" whispered to Marvin.

Marvin accepted the suggestion and stood.

After several lines of "Lord, we thank Thee," there was the scraping of chairs and the sound of voices that signaled the beginning of the meal.

Maryland ripe tomato juice with a slice of lemon was the first item on the menu. Momentarily there was hesitation about what to do with the lemon. Bite it? Save it? Squeeze it? We followed the example of our hosts and squeezed it into the juice. Brian Spitzer preferred his tomato juice straight—so he tried a shot of lemon at Neil Machen. The master, whose name was Mr. Willens, suggested, "If you have no taste for lemons, it would be appropriate to leave the slice on your plate."

There was that definite feeling in the air that Mr. Willens was prepared to ask us questions to "bring us out." But fortunately Jerry Trout was studying the walls looking for oleo stains. The master must have thought Jerry wanted to know more about the plaques. That was all the cue he needed to tell us about the Latin School's lacrosse team. It seems lacrosse was their sport and the one in which Mr. Willens had a particular interest. Phillip Moore knew all about the Johns Hopkins' teams which had won the national championship.

Phillip recited the names of the Hopkins all-American attack and Mr. Willens identified the fellows in his class who had gone on to coach college teams. The lunch was going along pretty well until a fellow asked for the bread tray. It was a kind of straw basket lined with a napkin and it was in front of me. I noticed it was empty. That wouldn't have been particularly important except that Bloom was sitting right next to the fellow who had requested the bread and Marvin had three rolls on his bread-and-butter

173

plate in addition to a couple of slices of white bread waiting on the table in reserve.

Mr. Willens had no way of knowing that even though Marvin was big for his age, all he ever brought for lunch was rolls which he ate along with the free milk.

Everyone at our table was quiet. Mr. Willens hinted that perhaps the fellow requesting the bread could "make a loan from the boy who is stocking inventory to open a bakery." Marvin wasn't pleased with himself for sitting before the prayer and now that he was caught cold in another breach of Mr. Muncrief's "discipline and manners," all Marvin could do was ignore the master and try to make the whole thing disappear. He tried to do this by swallowing a roll in a gulp. A second roll was poised in one hand while with the other Marvin made an effort to shield his bread plate from our stares.

No one could think of a thing to say to divert attention from Marvin. All eyes were glued on him. Would he knock off the rolls gulp by gulp? Did he plan to eliminate the bread in a similar manner? Or would Marvin Bloom change his mind and share his booty with the fellow from the Latin School?

But Marvin Bloom wasn't exactly the kind of fellow who talked his way out of a tight spot. When cornered, Marvin closed his eyes and swung. With two rolls gone and only one remaining, Marvin seemed about to create another legend to hold its place with the class of '42's oleo caper.

Marvin needed time to save himself, and Homer Fink came to the rescue. *"Duas tantum res anxius optat. Panem et circenses,"* said Homer. It meant absolutely nothing to us, but there was no denying the ponderous tone of Homer's voice. Several of the Latin boys were about to rise to their feet as if in response to another prayer. Mr. Willens was delighted. "Precisely. Absolutely to the point."

Wally volunteered that the last two words meant "bread and circus games." They got to conjugating and declining—all that stuff that sends our ninth-graders flying from Latin into Spanish. But it worked. While all the talking was going on, Marvin Bloom quietly offered his bread tray to his neighbor. Homer Fink had saved our school's reputation. But that was before the main course.

23

BALTIMORE IS FAMOUS for being a seafood town. I don't know that for a fact. I mean from personal experience. The truth is I have only been out of the United States once and that was on a weekend trip to Quebec, Canada, when I was ten years old. We stayed at a big hotel that looked like a fort. When we registered, I was standing right next to my father. There was no doubt he wrote "Baltimore" plainly and clearly, but all the clerk said was, "With your brood I suppose you'll be needing two connecting rooms." Not a word about Baltimore's soft-shell crabs or oysters or Potomac herring.

None of the fellows at camp mentioned it either. There were boys from Philadelphia and

Wilmington, Richmond, and New York City. They would talk about the Colts and the Orioles and when we had the camp quiz contest someone asked a question about the home of "The Star-Spangled Banner." That was the only time Baltimore ever came up. I could have come from Cleveland or Dallas, Texas, for all they mentioned seafood. The reason I know Baltimore is famous for seafood is that my Uncle Harry, who lives in Salt Lake City, says so. Whenever Uncle Harry comes to visit he tells my dad right off, "Let's go to the Chesapeake or Pimlico House and get some seafood. No place in the world makes crab cakes as good as they do in good old Bawlermuh," (Uncle Harry says it just like that. He always makes a big thing about how we say the name of our town. It splits him up.)

Baltimore may be famous for seafood, but Homer Fink is the only fellow my age who would rather eat crab cakes than hamburgers.

The only kind of fish they served at P.S. 79's cafeteria was fried scallops. We ate them with ketchup, and the way they were battered and fried they tasted like French fried potatoes. I don't know who made the menus at the Latin School, but they sure didn't know much about the eating habits of public school boys. We could smell fish the minute the waiters brought the trays from the kitchen. A big white hunk was sitting in the middle of each dish,

177

all dolled up with chopped parsley, mashed potatoes, and Brussels sprouts. They must have been on sale all over town that week.

Across the table from me Brian Spitzer was rolling his eyes and nodding his head. There was no doubt about the message. Brian was no fonder of fish than I was. (Sometimes in the spring I would eat baked shad if my mother picked out all the bones.)

Neil Machen was exchanging pained stares with Jerry Trout. And Little Louie Bannerman said, "Fish is brain food. It certainly is brain food. Very good for you." But his fork progressed no further than the mashed potatoes.

"I always get a little tense before a game," Phillip Moore said to Oliver. "And I have no appetite."

That was good thinking on Phillip's part, but it wasn't an excuse we could all use.

"Mr. Muncrief was in great form, the other day," Brian Spitzer reminded us. "I know I'm never going to forget the wonderful advice he gave us."

"Me either," said Neil and he tried a small piece of fish and a larger swallow of water.

"Excellent fillet," said Mr. Willens.

Homer Fink had a Latin quote handy that immediately absorbed the master in a discussion of Juvenal.

I watched as Wally forked a Brussels sprout

and ate it. He followed with a slice of fish, then another sprout. He said to me, "Chef is putting his best foot forward in honor of our guests."

Oliver agreed the fish was particularly tasty. The battle-lines were drawn and the boys of 79 had been ambushed. Not only were we confronted with an impossible menu, but in the face of our host's enthusiasm, there seemed no way to put the dish aside.

Finally, in desperation, I shred and spread the white fish and buried it under the mashed potatoes. No one would ever know what was in those small hills spaced at irregular intervals on the large plate. Brian Spitzer took the cue from me and Jerry Trout followed Brain. At the other end of the table I could see Little Louie Bannerman cautiously storing what was left of his fish portion into the fluffy potato mass.

I was proud of the popularity of my idea, but I could think of nothing to do with the Brussels sprouts.

Marvin Bloom had a sprout on his fork and he was struggling to be brave. I guess Marvin was trying to make up for the roll scene. He put the sprout to his mouth, rolled it briefly to smother the flavor, and managed miraculously to swallow it.

That was not the solution for me. I looked up and down the table in search of an alternative.

Little Louie Bannerman extracted a thin leaf, made a sandwich out of it, and polished it off with a long drink of milk. It was a possibility but one that would attract too much attention.

Our last hope was that Homer Fink would have an inspiration. I knew from visits to the Fink house that Homer ate broccoli and cauliflower, eggplant, and okra. In the spring he was delirious about fresh asparagus. Sure enough, Homer was eating the fish and sprouts, and from his expression it was obvious the chef's time was not wasted on him. There seemed to be no choice but to throw in the napkin. Again Little Louie reminded us of Mr. Muncrief's warning. None of us wanted to sacrifice our varsity sports program. As a last resort I tried to get a message through to Homer.

While Mr. Willens was directing a waiter to refill the milk pitcher I said, "Brother Pete. Him flip. Brussels sprout." I rubbed my stomach and licked my lips.

Homer Fink's eyes darted from me to my platter and then quickly he surveyed the rest of the table. It was a problem involving the honor of the school. Its political repercussions could be enormous.

"Scratchy head. Think um hard," I told my candidate.

"Me savvy," said Homer Fink and in the next instant the Fink napkin trick was born. It was simple, but I guess geniuses see the obvious.

"Baby cabbages, Papoose. Pronto," said Homer. Then raising a sprout high with his fork, he exclaimed, *"Omni. Omni."*

As Mr. Willens corrected Homer's pronunciation and recited the first chapter of Caesar's *Gallic War,* Homer Fink, with a flourish of the fork, deposited the first sprout in the napkin resting in his lap.

"Great!" said Brian Spitzer.

"Thank you," replied Mr. Willens, unaware that Brian was commenting on Homer's trick.

"More. More," was the clamor from Neil Machen.

Mr. Willens continued reciting, but Homer Fink would not do an encore. Prodding Mr. Willens with phrases and sentences, Homer concentrated upon the master's performance and his own dish of Brussels sprouts which he seemed to be enjoying immensely.

Caesar was telling us about the brave Belgae when the last of the P.S. 79 sprouts were evacuated. Again, we received our cue from Homer Fink. It was Homer who first rolled the napkin into a ball and deposited it with its sacred cargo into his back pocket.

After tapioca and cookies, Louie Bannerman thanked our hosts for a memorable meal.

24

THE LATIN SCHOOL TEAM turned out for the game dressed in uniforms. They had on short pants and numbered jerseys and knee-length socks and shoes made for playing soccer. We were wearing khaki pants and gray sweat shirts and most of the fellows wore their sneakers for speed, even though Mr. Muncrief had advised us that a solid leather toe was preferred for kicking.

What we lacked in equipment we made up for with our cheering section. Trudy Deal had convinced half a dozen girls to show up in their togas and Elaine Steigmar carried a huge megaphone. Every time the girls in togas led a cheer they leaped into the air, togas flying.

The Latin School's rooters sat quietly in their blazers and poplin raincoats. Occasionally they applauded, but through the opening ceremonies they were absorbed watching P.S. 79's cheerleaders.

"Two. Four. Six. Eight," Elaine screamed. And the girls in togas joined her. "Whom do we appreciate?"

There was some confusion during the response. "Lafayette—Lafayette," the better-disciplined fans answered. But from both sides of the field came the reply, "Homer Fink."

Before the kickoff, each of the Latin School's players greeted his opposite number from Lafayette. They shook our hands and wished us well and the game was on.

Less than five minutes after the opening gun the Latins executed a smooth pass play that brought the ball deep into our territory. They kicked off and pushed the ball back to the left half. Immediately Wally, their center forward, set off for the left wing as though the ball were already on its way there. Brian Spitzer chased after after him and had gone fifteen yards before realizing his mistake. He turned to fill the gap he had left in the middle but was too late to cut off a ground pass to Oliver, the inside right, who had moved into the center forward. Phillip Moore made a desperate try to block the goal, but the Latins scored.

The host's rooting section greeted the goal with a light clap of hands. It was obvious they were saving their energy for a long afternoon.

Phillip Moore made four saves before the Latins scored again. Their third goal came on a play set up by Oliver who ran left and passed right. Again deserted by the defense, Phillip Moore could do nothing to counter the boot.

It seemed our fans were going to have nothing more to cheer than Phillip Moore's one-man effort. But in the opening seconds of the third quarter Neil Machen tried a long kick from midfield. Neil's foot went back and shot forward with all his strength. The ball was stolen from under him and Neil went flying into the air, landing smack on his bottom. When he stood, there was a wide green stain on his rear pocket.

The umpire suggested, "Either this boy has chlorophyl running in his veins or a pocketful of green ink."

Neil urged that the game be continued.

Perhaps it was our growing frustration. Maybe it was because of our exhaustion. But during the third quarter Trout and Spitzer, Bloom, and finally Little Louie himself were seated on the Latin School's turf. When each boy stood to resume play there was a similar green stain on the rear of his pants.

The Latin School rooters tried to muffle their delight, but our public school fans were not nearly as restrained. Each time one of our players hit the dirt, the girls in togas led a vigorous cheer. It was all we had to cheer for—we may not have been winning the game, but certainly no one ever played soccer more colorfully.

While all this was going on the inventor himself was patrolling his position at right fullback. With his hands clasped behind his back, Homer Fink walked back and forth deep in concentration.

During the third-quarter break Little Louie urged, "Get on the ball, Homer. Give it a try. You haven't kicked the ball even once."

Phillip Moore was quick to come to Homer's defense. "Homer thinks best under pressure. I hope you are considering the waste problems as it relates to world poverty, Homer."

To me Homer Fink confided, "Let us put away Marx and Freud and ponder beauty and truth with ferocity."

"While you're being ferocious, how about giving the ball a boot once in a while, Homer," I said. "You'll never win an election unless you prove a little school spirit."

"What is the school in the abstract?" said Homer. "It has no meaning, no identity apart from that we as individuals impose upon it. Which is all the more reason for us to champion the individual."

I could see Homer was in the mood for one of

his Plato discussions and with the team trailing by three goals and a rout in progress, I decided it was best not to debate the point.

Little Louie continued his pep talk. "At least let's keep them from a shutout," said the team captain. "We can score a moral victory."

"Morals are made of sterner stuff," countered Homer.

"Can't I take this mush out of my back pocket?" asked Marvin Bloom.

We were all agreed that was not possible.

"I feel as if I'm playing soccer in a bathing suit," Neil Machen said. "But what else can we do?"

The third quarter began with another Latin score. From his position at right fullback I heard Homer advise the Latin fans near him to "think before it is too late."

I managed to sidle near Homer long enough to urge him again to give the ball a boot. "At least show them you're trying."

But for all the discouragement on our side the Latin boys were more concerned with Homer Fink than the game. A group patrolled the sidelines in step with Homer, hands clasped behind their backs, chanting, "Think with Fink."

I guess it would have gone on like that until the end of the game, but suddenly the ball was in Homer's area of the field. Players rushed toward it. Homer Fink stepped aside ignoring the action.

He was deep in thought and did not wish to be interrupted.

"Homer Fink has no guts," I heard Brian Spitzer say. "He's afraid to try to score a goal so he's trying to save the world."

Even the girls in togas were becoming impatient with Homer. Chanting, "Go, Fink, go," their voices were louder than the Latin rooters urging, "Think with Fink." It was easy enough to encourage someone to think when he was on the other team and you were ahead by four goals.

Little Louie got to the ball first and he trapped it with the sole of his foot. He passed it to Marvin Bloom who gave it a great boot. Marvin's kick was wild. The ball was moving to the sidelines where it would certainly go off sides and the Latins would then be given possession. Only Homer Fink stood between the ball and the sidelines. His eyes were lowered and his back hunched. There was no telling how many centuries past he was entertaining—what realms of thoughts he was invading.

"Your head. Use your head, Homer," I called to him.

These were the same words Homer had used on the day previous when fresh with discovery and reading he was enthusiastic about soccer. Homer Fink raised his head, jumped in the air, and met the ball squarely with his forehead. It bounded down the field toward the Latin School's goal. Little Louie raced after it and with a diagonal boot saved us from a shutout.

The girls in togas leaped into the air. Even the Latin School cheered Homer's pass. It was as if Little Louie Bannerman had no part in the score. The glory was all Homer's. He had delivered a powerful head pass. The referee delayed the game and called for a towel to wipe the smudge from Homer's forehead.

"I'm all right," Homer Fink reassured the referee.

"You seem to have a bruise," the older man insisted.

"It's just dirt," said Homer Fink. And then to prove it he reached into his rear pocket for a handkerchief to wipe the spot from his forehead.

Three more minutes were left in the game. But no one scored. No one cared any longer about the game. We were all too busy laughing because Homer Fink had no handkerchief in his pants pocket—only a napkin. And when he pulled it out there was no mistaking what bounded on the field—a big ripe green Brussels sprout.

25

I WAS TOO BUSY chasing the Latin players who were kicking the soccer ball all afternoon to have noticed the photographers. But Saturday morning there was a two-column picture on the back page of the morning *Sun*. Several of the girls from 79 dressed in togas were gathered around a fellow in a poplin raincoat holding a big sign that said, THINK WITH FINK.

SCHOOL BOY URGES RETURN TO CLASSICS, the headline read.

Homer Fink, son of Dr. Alcibiades X. Fink, member of the classics department of Johns Hopkins University, advocates that schoolboys and girls unite to 'contemplate truth and justice' in the classic tradition of Greek philosophers. Young Fink is a candidate for the presidency of the student council of P.S. 79. According to the demonstration yesterday afternoon he has an enthusiastic following at the neighboring Latin School.

The story went on to tell that the soccer game had become a rally for Fink and it mentioned that the slogan "Think with Fink" had mysteriously appeared on school walls and blackboards in places as distant as Dundalk and Glen Burnie.

There was a quote from Oliver explaining, "Homer Fink has given us a rallying cry more meaningful than winning the next football game."

"I'm tired of blue jeans," an unnamed girl was quoted as saying. "When I wear a toga I feel like I really stand for something."

On the inside page jump was a small picture of Homer holding the napkin to his forehead. He had a warm, kind of surprised smile on his face. The Brussels sprout appeared as a blur. There were quotes from Homer in Latin and Greek and a testimony from Little Louie Bannerman whom the story reported had a strong following in his own bid for the student-council presidency. "I am not opposed to truth or justice," Little Louie was reported as saying, "but it is my belief that Fink is a little over his head. I would rather concentrate on an after-school athletic program and measures to prevent juvenile delinquency."

The delinquency issue was a new feature of the Bannerman campaign and I took it as a sign that Little Louie was running scared.

"Congratulations," my father said. "You're certainly pulling out all the stops. Why, Homer Fink will be on his way to Annapolis at the speed you're going."

I explained to my father that I had been too busy being a good sport, shaking the Latin players' hands, and cleaning up the field to even know there had been a reporter at the game. But I delayed my pancakes and bacon and went to the telephone to call Homer.

The line was busy for a while, but finally Homer's mother answered. She was polite but a little rushed. Mrs. Fink wasn't trying to impress me with how busy she was. I don't think the Finks believed it was possible to send the sound of a voice over a wire. Mr. Fink always spoke slowly and clearly selecting each word as though he were composing a poem. Mrs. Fink sounded as if she wanted to get the talking over with before the instrument exploded.

I told her about the story in the paper and what a famous man Homer had become. She thanked me. "Mr. Fink and I are so grateful to you, Richard. You've been a marvelous friend to Homer. You must visit us soon and we'll have a long talk and special dinner with all the foods you like best. Now here's Homer."

Homer was less impressed. "It's the idea, not the man who is important," he told me. "Besides I'm not so sure I'm temperamentally equipped for politics. The phone has been ringing all morning. I don't have time to think."

I told Homer it was a small sacrifice to make for public responsibility. He answered by saying, "Power corrupts men." Then he went on to cite examples from history.

"But you've been called, Homer," I reminded him. "Remember Pan and Silenus and Mr. Muncrief and the mouse. Maybe the gods are just testing you. You can't quit now."

Homer Fink didn't answer that. "I need time to contemplate," he said. "I'm not answering any more calls. I have to think."

"There's nothing to think about," I said. "You're running for the presidency of the school and you have Phillip Moore and me working with all our might to get you elected. The least you can do is answer a few telephone calls and keep the voters happy for one more week."

"I'm not certain Socrates and Pericles could have exchanged roles," was Homer's answer. "It may well be that a philosopher is not equipped by temperament for the demands of leadership."

"Knock it off, Homer. You're not Socrates or Pericles, and all that stuff about the gods is only in your mind. What's real is the election. You got a great break with that story in the paper this morning. And I don't exactly feel like begging you to take advantage of it."

"You're a better friend than I deserve," Homer Fink said gently. "But I must decide this by myself."

"I'll see you in school," I said. "And you'd better be ready to shake some hands and make a few speeches. Every schoolboy in town is ready to trade rock-and-roll records for a Plato pony. That was your idea, not mine. And you'd better be there to explain it."

"We'll see," said Homer Fink and he quoted Greek again.

Before I hung up I said, "Be there Monday. I don't care how many dirty garbage cans you sit in over the weekend."

My mother made a fresh batch of griddle cakes but I wasn't hungry.

Pete saw Homer's picture and said, *"Omni— 'Omni—,"* and I told him to shut up.

26

ALL DAY MONDAY students were reacting to the newspaper story. Patty Esposito told me on the way to math class that a group of girls had organized a city-wide toga committee. "We tried to limit ourselves, but Elaine has a cousin in Roland Park and Trudy's friend who lives in Ruxton wants to join us."

I agreed as long as everyone realized the importance of togas to the Fink campaign. Patty said, "Of course." But when I asked for an example, she said, "Togas have to do with culture and thinking about things that are ancient and intellectual like Homer Fink." I reminded Patty that her committee should involve girls from our school who could vote.

During the library period Neil Machen put aside a history of the battles of the Second World War to read the story of the *Iliad*. Neil told me, "If Homer Fink is right, Mars could have been General George S. Patton during the Battle of the Bulge."

I told Neil not to let that get around. "The main thing is to get people thinking like the ancient Greeks, not necessarily fighting like them."

The situation got a little out of control during biology class. Mr. Bowen was instructing us on the dissection of a frog. He had a chart on the board pointing out the cranial chest and tubercles. We were going to hack away until we found "a few short ribs."

"I'm not cutting anything," Brian Spitzer announced. "What's chopping up a frog have to do with truth and justice?"

"Science has led us down a blind alley," chimed in Jerry Trout. "The atomic bomb got us mass suicide."

"Where's Homer?"

"We want to hear from Homer Fink," the other voices agreed.

But Homer wasn't in school and Mr. Bowen had trouble understanding the argument.

"Scientists constantly search for truth," our biology teacher insisted. "When we examine the anatomical composition of the frog we take the first step to understanding the structure of the human body."

Jerry Trout wasn't convinced. "We want Latin. We want Greek."

"Give us Socrates. Let's read Plato," Brian continued. "Think with Fink."

Mr. Bowen spent the remainder of the period explaining how the early Greeks began biology. He told us about a Greek named Alcmaeon who began the investigation of animal structure.

On our way to the next class Phillip Moore said to me, "At this stage of the campaign, every day is crucial. Without Homer the issues get confused."

"Every knock is a boost," I reassured Phillip. But I wasn't convinced. Remembering my conversation with Homer on the telephone, I was sure he was off somewhere—contemplating.

At the end of the school day students from all over the city gathered in our yard to meet Homer. Wally and Oliver led a group from the Latin School, and there were girls anxious to get to work on the toga committee. Several boys from East Baltimore came with their shoelaces untied and their shirttails out. Word had gotten around that Homer recommended contemplation in a garbage can and a boy from Garrison rode over on his bicycle dragging a G.I. can behind him.

"It's just wonderful," Patty Esposito said to me. "Everyone loves Homer. He'll win the election for sure." Then she said, "Remember that cute little boy running down the isle. I hear he's Homer's brother and he was born speaking Latin. It runs in the family."

Somebody started chanting, "Think with Fink." And then a boy from the Latin School turned the G.I. can upside down, stood on top of it, and led a cheer. "*Amo, amas. Amamus Fink.*"

It caught on and soon the whole yard was echoing the conjugation of the verb "to love" with Homer's name as the object.

With so many rumors, issues, and philosophies making the rounds, Homer's campaign was building its own momentum. I was just beginning to enjoy running a campaign without a candidate when Little Louie Bannerman asked for equal time on the garbage can.

Neil Machen protested and even Brian Spitzer seemed reluctant to let Little Louie have the floor. But Phillip Moore reminded everyone that conflicting views were the strength of a democracy and he prepared the way for Little Louie.

"I'm certainly not against Homer's program for a return to the classics," Little Louie reassured us. "A doctor can't write prescriptions without Latin."

That was greeted by applause and a new call for Homer Fink.

Little Louie's face was flushed and for the first time in the campaign there was a tremble to his voice. He must have known as well as the rest of us that he was not campaigning against a boy any longer. At that moment Homer Fink was as close as a schoolboy at P.S. 79 could come to having his own private seat right up there on Olympus.

Impatiently, the boys from other schools objected to Louie's starched shirt. Someone sneered, "You can't trust him. He uses Vitalis." Others voiced suspicion because Little Louie's shoes were shined. He had made his testimonial to Homer and now they wanted Louie Bannerman to step down.

Again Phillip Moore protected Louie Bannerman's right to have his say.

"Friends, classmates, fellow students," Little Louie pleaded. "I'm not here to debate with Homer Fink. I dig him."

Little Louie wasn't the kind of boy you would expect to understand a word like "dig," much less to use it. The audience quieted. It was obvious to me Little Louie had been thinking long and hard all weekend—and probably getting some grown-up political advice too. He went on to praise the things Homer had done for our school. Most particularly, he cited

Homer's performance in the soccer game and the debt we all owed Homer for "getting us to think about really important things."

Standing tall on the garbage can, Little Louie Bannerman came to the heart of his speech—the really important part that I knew right away was meant to make the voters doubt Homer. "I'm for truth and justice," explained Little Louie, "but whatever the results of this election may be we must not forget—*home*—and *mother*—and *pets*."

There was a groan from some parts of the yard, but applause too. Moving quickly, I approached Phillip Moore. "You'd better talk next," I urged Phillip. "Give them world poverty and doing our part to save the peace. I'll try to contact Homer."

As I started out of the yard, Phillip Moore was talking. I heard him telling Homer's fans about ways to save wax paper from sandwich wrappings and "making a friend a year in an underdeveloped country to save the peace." Phillip was tying the whole thing in with the Greeks' respect for the individual, and the girls in togas were jumping up and down screaming, "Score with Moore."

27

I WENT TO HOMER FINK'S HOUSE.
I was going to tell him how important it
was for him to return to school. There was
no doubt in my mind that with Little Louie
Bannerman and Phillip Moore taking turns on
the platform, by Friday many of the voters
would forget all about the living legend.

Homer was my friend, and regardless of how
difficult he was at times, I felt I owed it to him
to make one last effort to get him back into
the campaign. Homer had entered our routine
school election and turned it into a city-wide
movement. There was some confusion about
his platform, and half the kids who were
screaming didn't have the least idea what they
were screaming about. But I remembered the
dullness of past campaigns and the uneasy feeling of boys like Phillip Moore who wanted to be

involved in something important and never had the chance until Homer Fink had started to talk.

It seemed to me we needed Homer. And Homer needed us. He had told me P.S. 79 would be in his base. I was convinced that without us he would be another daydreamer, tripping over his shoelaces. I was even beginning to feel as if I were on a historic mission. Homer Fink needed me the way all great men needed a friend. I was ready to beg, argue, even fight, if necessary, to get him back into the race.

Professor Fink greeted me at the door. He was wearing slippers and a vest sprinkled with pipe ashes. His glasses were low on his nose and in one hand he held a book.

"Welcome, Richard." He clasped my forearm.

Homer's father wasn't usually in a talkative mood, but I could see this was a time when he welcomed company. When I asked for Homer, the Professor told me, "Homer is not about." He invited me in to share a pomegranate and followed him to the kitchen.

The Professor's back was to me as he leaned into the refrigerator. He couldn't see my expression when he said, "I'm delighted you dropped by, Richard. Perhaps you can help solve the riddle of Homer's sudden interest in the Romantic poets."

"Romantic?" I could feel the blood rush to my face.

"Keats, Shelley, Wordsworth," said the Professor. "The chief authors of the late eighteenth and early nineteenth century were Romantics."

In a voice that was barely a whisper I said, "Homer Fink's in love." I didn't wait for the pomegranate. "Excuse me. Some other time, sir. I have to be getting home."

The Professor was still searching for the fruit when I heard him say, "Of course Romanticism is not a systematic philosophy, but an intuitive faith. . . ."

"Good-by," I said from the door.

I went to Goldenheimer's and had a double-scoop hot fudge sundae with whipped cream, and when Mrs. Goldenheimer was wiping the table and filling the sugar bowls I asked if she had a telephone book. She brought me one from the back and told me that even though they made it a point not to have a public telephone, for a good customer like me they would make an exception. She offered me the use of the store phone. I thanked her and explained I was just checking an address.

Mrs. Goldenheimer looked a little confused. "Suit yourself. Cha. Cha. Cha."

I took the crosstown and then the Charles Street bus. It was late afternoon by the time I arrived at Katrinka Nonningham's. The sun was shaded by a cloud in the west and the big trees on Howard's Lane were gray and bare, I walked up and down the block and thought once more about finding a public phone and calling. Finally I walked right up the path to Katrinka's front door. There was no bell, but a large brass knocker. It was stiff and made a soft thudding sound that I was sure no one inside could hear. I knocked twice and a man in a starched white jacket with a black bowtie answered. I told him I'd come to see Katrinka. He asked my name, directed me in, and said, "Madam will be with you shortly."

In the hall there were two armless chairs covered by a fabric that looked like silk. I was certain if I sat I would leave a permanent impression in them. My bookbag was tucked tightly under my arm and I searched for something to look at to seem busy. There was only the crystal chandelier and a gold-framed mirror, so I stood absolutely still.

After several seconds I heard a door open and then the tinkling of glasses and the sound of polite conversation. A woman's voice said, "Yes?"

Across the hall I saw a tall, beautiful lady. Her hair was swept up high on her head and a jeweled comb was in the midst of it. She was wearing the kind of dress my mother only put on for weddings and from the way she was standing I knew she had come as far as she ever would to greet anyone.

I told her, "I'd like to see Katrinka."

The woman said nothing, but just looked at me. I thought for a moment I had the wrong house and I was going to excuse myself and leave.

"Katrinka?" the woman repeated. "You mean Chookey. She's upstairs." There was a glassy look in the lady's eyes, as if she had come in from the sun or been crying.

I asked if I could see Katrinka.

"I suppose." And then the lady said, "It never rains but it pours." That made her laugh. I couldn't understand why. It didn't seem the kind of thing a beautiful lady who wore such an expensive dress in the middle of the afternoon would say. I started to the staircase.

When I had gone several steps she spoke again, "No doubt you've had the *mea-sles*." She made it sound like something dirty, but I admitted I had.

At the top of the stairs was a long hall with paintings on the walls. I would have liked to look at them, so I could tell my parents. But when I reached the top step I heard a familiar voice and hurried toward the direction from which it came.

The door was slightly ajar. I looked in and saw Katrinka sitting up in bed with two pillows behind her head. She was wearing a plaid woolen bathrobe like the one my father had given me for Christmas and her hair was loose and falling forward on her face. The shades were drawn, but I could see Katrinka's face clearly. There were faint blotches about her cheeks and chin.

"This was Hector's prayer for his son," I heard Homer Fink say. "It's part of his moving farewell to Andromache, his wife." Homer started to recite from the *Iliad*.

I stood by the door to Katrinka Nonningham's bedroom and listened. Homer's voice was stronger than I had ever heard it. There was a musical quality about his recitation as if he were chanting a prayer that was every word the truth and the listener had better pay attention to understand the mysteries of life. After reciting a while, Homer translated and he explained the story to Katrinka.

Several times I heard Homer say, "You must know Aphrodite. You must remember."

Katrinka Nonningham's eyes were half-closed. She seemed drowsy and I saw her head bob. "Go on," she whispered to Homer. "Please go on."

As Homer repeated more of the *Iliad* Katrinka Nonningham reached to her night table and poured a glass of apple juice. She was having some difficulty controlling the pitcher and

I wanted to help. But there was a spell in the room and I could not intrude.

Homer was telling Katrinka about a translator named Chapman and a poem of Keats. I heard him recite:

> Much have I travell'd in the realms of gold,
>> And many goodly states and kingdoms seen;
>> Round many western islands have I been
> Which bards in fealty to Apollo hold.

Homer made it sound as if the words came directly from his own heart and I believed him, even though I know the only place he had ever visited was Ocean City.

Katrinka Nonningham fumbled with the pillow. I thought she was going for a handkerchief because she was moved to tears. But she located a pair of sun glasses and put them on. When Homer said:

> Then felt I like some watcher of the skies
>> When a new planet swims into his ken . . .

I knew exactly how John Keats felt. Only it wasn't the *Iliad* that was turning me on. It was Katrinka Nonningham. With her dark glasses, wool bathrobe, and measles I was absolutely positive she wasn't a goddess at all. It was as though I were seeing her for the first time. Katrinka Nonningham was a girl my age having a tough time at home. She was sad and lonely and needed a boy friend.

Homer continued reciting but I didn't hear another word he said. I just stood and looked at Katrinka. Finally her head slumped forward.

Homer rose from his chair and went to her. I felt a weakness about my knees. I was sure if I had even a little character I would turn away and leave. Homer had probably been visiting Katrinka all afternoon, keeping her company through the measles, and I knew it was none of my business how he was rewarded for it.

I saw Homer stand by the bed and slowly remove a pillow from beneath the perfect golden head. He pulled the pink spread close to Katrinka's chin and then Homer Fink returned to his chair and continued to recite.

On the way home I thought about what my mother had meant when she said, "Some children pass from childhood into adolescence more slowly than others." I was wondering if Homer Fink was still a child or if perhaps, genius that he was, he had skipped adolescence and plunged right into being an old man.

Greek and Latin and even the entire first team of the Romantic poets weren't going to get him any closer to Katrinka Nonningham. It seemed to me Homer Fink needed to win the school election more than he or I realized.

In the meantime I made up my mind to ask Katrinka for a real date. And I didn't plan to prepare myself by reading poetry.

28

HOMER DIDN'T RETURN to school Tuesday. I called him that evening to let him know Little Louie Bannerman was getting support from the Boy Scout troop. "Little Louie's also picking up help from the kids who sing in the church glee club," I informed Homer. "And he's recommending we organize a pet club for the protection of stray dogs and cats."

Homer cautioned me to warn the students about Little Louie's commitment to vivisection. "Find out what he intends doing with the stray pets," said Homer. "Doctors will traditionally murder to dissect."

I suggested that Homer could make an issue of that point more easily than I could. "Why don't you pop into class tomorrow and let the kids know you're still around."

Homer said he was occupied with "personal commitments." If he didn't want to tell me about Katrinka Nonningham, I wasn't going to press him. Even the *Iliad* has to end some time, I thought, and I wondered what Homer would perform next. The more I considered, the more convinced I was that there was no end to Homer's readings and recitations—so Wednesday I called Katrinka.

I didn't say anything about the election. I didn't even mention the women's committee. I told Katrinka I was sorry to hear she had the measles and I asked her when she thought she would be up and around again. Her doctor had given her permission to go out on the weekend, but Katrinka told me she doubted if she would look well enough to see people.

I suggested we take a walk. "I've seen measles lots of times," I said. "I had them and so did Pete. You haven't seen anything until you've seen a redhead with red spots."

That made her laugh and Katrinka agreed she could stand it if I could. "It's wonderful about Homer," she said. "With all the stories about him in the papers I'm sure he'll win the election."

I said, "I'll see you Saturday and tell you all about it."

Thursday morning Homer was accompanied to school by his mother. After a long conference in Mr. Muncrief's office, he returned to class.

"How did you talk your way out of that one?" I asked Homer during lunch hour. "Did you tell Mr. Muncrief you were absent because you were sick? Or was your grandmother dying?"

Homer disapproved of both standard excuses. According to him, "such fabrications tempt the wrath of the gods."

I had heard all I cared to hear about the gods. They seemed to have deserted Homer at a crucial time in the election, and as far as I was concerned they were a luxury he could no longer afford.

"I explained to Mr. Muncrief that I was comforting a stray and wounded creature," said Homer Fink. "Another Persephone."

"That's blackmail, Homer." And then I smiled, "You know you may make a politician after all. You're learning."

Phillip Moore was less confident. "Convince Homer to speak at the meeting this afternoon," Phillip told me. "Fink chapters from all over the city are clamoring for a statement of objectives. If Homer doesn't show, we'll have to proceed without him."

210

I explained to Phillip Moore that I was more concerned with having Homer rally the local students. "Little Louie is pumping some hot issues. Between dogs, and mothers, and home, he has a little something for everybody."

Phillip Moore confessed to an interest greater than the campaign. "It seems to me the contribution Homer Fink has made goes far beyond the schoolyard of P.S. 79. We have the makings of an international student crusade."

I listened to Phillip Moore go on about the great issues of our time. He was so sincere, so dedicated. He sounded even more convinced than Homer Fink that he could change the world.

"We have something so old it's fresh and exciting," said Phillip. "The concept of the individual as introduced by the Greeks is the truth we need to fight the materialism in the world today."

I listened a while longer and then I said, "Why don't you draw up the statement of objectives, Phillip? Homer's not available and I'm sure there's no one he knows who understands him as well as you do."

"But it was Homer's idea," said Phillip. "He deserves the honor of leading us.

"You'd be doing Homer a great favor, Phillip. Our man has his hands full winning this election. And just between you and me—I'm not even sure he wants to win."

"I don't understand," said Phillip Moore. "Homer cared enough to make the speech at the terminal. He wanted to run for the presidency. He asked us to support him."

I shrugged my shoulders and then I said, "That's the way it goes sometimes Phillip. I wanted to be a policeman before I grew up."

My answer wasn't enough for Phillip Moore. I could see he was thinking hard. And then he said with a relieved smile, "Homer Fink must be writing a book. He's putting it all down in black and white. Pretty soon they'll be hearing from him all over the world."

"In the meantime you get the crusade going," I said. "I'm going to talk to Homer about bringing Argus to school. It's time that mutt made himself useful."

29

I WAS WASTING MY TIME.

When they gathered around him after school, clamoring for a final speech, Homer explained he had to be on his way. "It's traditional on the eve of great events to visit the Oracle of Delphi."

Elaine Steigmar thought that was "cute." And Marvin Bloom said, "Homer Fink has better sense than to waste his afternoon arguing with Louie Bannerman when he could be playing ball." Neil Machen wanted to know what the Oracle was and I explained that it seemed to be a kind of poll announced in riddles.

But Little Louie made a big point out of Homer's absence from school. Without accusing Homer directly, he implied that his opponent was encouraging school dropouts. There was no great cheering for Little Louie, but the students listened to him. What he lacked in color he made up for with work. Little Louie spoke about delinquency. He said all the things we'd heard a hundred times, but he sounded as if he cared.

Little Louie was back to discussing the noise in the school cafeteria when I grasped Brian Spitzer by the sleeve. Sleeving is a great thing in politics. When you want somebody to do something for you, you pull him gently by the sleeve and talk in whispers as if the whole thing is very confidential and involves a great trust. I guided Brian Spitzer to the back of the yard.

"As soon as Little Louie wraps this up, we'll give them a big 'Phooey to Louie,'" I told Brian. "Then you start them on 'Think with Fink.'"

"I'm not so sure," said Brian.

"What d'you mean—not sure?" I sleeved Brian again. "The kids are bored to death with Louie. They're just waiting for an excuse to start screaming for Homer."

"That may be," said Brian Spitzer. "But what I mean is I'm not so sure I'm for Homer any more."

I sleeved Brian really hard, pulling him up close and whispered into his ear, "Don't be ridiculous. There aren't a dozen students in this school who are going to vote for Bannerman. Why, Fink's practically a national institution."

214

"That's just it. That's the point," said Brian. "Where's he been all week? He comes to school one day and bing-bang he rushes to some oracle. It's just the calisthenics class and the soccer game all over again. Little Louie knocks himself out and Homer Fink gets all the attention."

I shook my head. "I'm disappointed in you, Brian. I'm beginning to have some doubts about Homer appointing you to the athletic committee."

"What athletic committee?"

"Homer racks his brains setting up an airtight organization for him and he asks what committee." I dropped my voice so low Brian could hardly hear. "Let me tell you—buzz buzz —a sports program that will be city-wide—buzz buzz—and you're the man to lead it. Those are Homer's very words."

Brian shook his arm loose and scratched his head. "I'd like to, Richard. Maybe if Homer were around a little more. But the way things stand right now—" Brian Spitzer looked toward Little Louie Bannerman who was back to harping on an after-school athletic program. "I know Little Louie is no match for Homer when it comes to brains, but to tell you the absolute truth—I'm not so sure I exactly go for all this thinking with Fink. What's it got me so far? I'm in hot water in biology class and stuck with two hours of Latin homework."

I didn't have to visit any oracles to see the signs of this election. Brian Spitzer told me all I needed to know.

When I called Homer's house that night, he didn't seem the least nervous and refused to discuss the election. "Good luck," I said before hanging up.

Homer's answer was, *"Contra felicem vix deus vires habet."* He didn't translate, but I wrote it down and found out later it meant, "Against a lucky man even a god has little power."

We voted by secret ballot. After writing the name of our choice on a two-by-four card, each student deposited his ballot in a box in the school auditorium. Phillip Moore acted as a poll watcher for Homer Fink, and at the last minute Neil Machen agreed to work for Little Louie.

Patty Esposito and Brian Spitzer represented the candidates as official tally clerks. The counting went on in Mr. Muncrief's office that afternoon. Neither Patty nor Brian returned to class, and we knew it was a very close election. Most of us remained in our homerooms after school waiting for the results.

Homer Fink preferred to receive the news in Druid Hill Park. "I'll be on Pan's hill," he told me. "Have no fears, Richard. I know I voted for the right man."

He walked across the schoolroom with his

hands stuffed deep into the pockets of his oversized overcoat. Several tattered books were under his arm—and I noticed the lace of his right shoe was coming undone.

At three-thirty we heard a great cheer in the hall. Rushing from our classroom, we received the news that a group was gathered in front of Mr. Muncrief's office. Mr. Aberdenally, the custodian, was standing there. The broomstick was in one hand and in the other hand the custodian held a mouse by the tail.

It relieved the tension of the election momentarily, and I guess I was grateful for that. But I heard myself say, "Rest in peace, Persephone."

The mouse had been hiding in the ballot box, one of the tellers told me later. She had revealed herself when Mr. Muncrief brought forth the last ballot.

Several minutes later the assistant principal appeared. It had been a very close election, he explained. "The ballots have been counted and recounted. There is no doubt. Elected by a plurality of one vote, the new president of the student body is—Louis Bannerman."

I thought I saw a tear in the corner of Mr. Muncrief's eye as he started down the hall to help Mr. Aberdenally dispose of the last remains of Persephone. I hurried to Druid Hill Park to tell the news to Homer Fink.

30

WHEN I ARRIVED AT THE HILL, Homer wasn't there. I found a piece of broken shoelace and saw the footprints of a small dog whom I knew must be Argus. Cupping my hands over my mouth I called, "Homer-rrr—Homer-rr. Fink-kkk." I was sure Homer was some place nearby, probably examining a bird nest or looking down a gopher hole. But there was no answer. It's just as well, I thought. I wasn't particularly looking forward to breaking the bad news.

I sat and twirled the strip of shoelace between my fingers. I tried to imagine how Homer had managed to step on his shoelace and break it without falling down. I remembered the lace of his right shoe was loose when he left school that afternoon and I regretted not having tied it for him. I wondered why I hadn't. At first, I thought it was because of the campaign. Things had changed between Homer and me since he decided to run for office. I considered the way Homer had walked out on the race and left me holding the bag.

I got to thinking about all I had done for Homer—organizing his campaign, putting up his signs, talking him up to the students. And then I considered the things Homer Fink had done for me. It isn't easy to understand the things people do for you. First of all you have to face the truth about yourself and nobody wants to admit that he isn't personally responsible for the best breaks in his life. Take me, for example. I had a date with Katrinka Nonningham all set for Saturday, and if things went well my prom date was going to be the kind of girl who was every boy's dream. I would have liked to think it was all due to my personality, my way with girls. But the truth was I couldn't even talk to Katrinka Nonningham if it hadn't been for Homer. She would have passed in and out of my life at the tennis courts.

Homer hadn't set out to bring us together, but it was because we both knew Homer Fink that Katrinka was prepared for me and I was able to understand her.

The more I thought about it the more convinced I was that Homer Fink had done something special for each of us who knew him. Phillip Moore may have been the best in everything without Homer, but it was because of Homer that Phillip finally found something to challenge him. The student crusade was right up Phillip Moore's alley, but nobody—not even Phillip himself—would have got it going if it hadn't been for Homer Fink.

Little Louie Bannerman was going to be a doctor and a pretty good one, judging from how serious he was about his homework and how energetic he'd been in the campaign. But I was certain, after his campaign with Homer, the world was never going to look the same to Little Louie. Some day when he was in a laboratory somewhere ready to start cutting up a dog or shoving needles into a cat, I was sure Little Louie would start thinking about "the order of the universe" or some other phrase of Homer Fink's that I never quite understood but which I was certain was very clear to a good science student like Little Louie.

And Brian Spitzer and Neil Machen and even Marvin Bloom would remember "truth and justice." All their lives they would be proud because Homer Fink had made them consider these things if only for a moment.

Trudy Deal, Alma Melchere, Patty Esposito, all the girls who had worn togas when others were showing off in tight blue jeans, would never be quite the same because of Homer. For a while they had belonged to a great and noble tradition that went all the way back to Socrates and the Roman Forum. No matter how you cut it, I'm sure all the girls of P.S. 79 realized they had shared, though briefly, a glimpse of a more enduring heritage than rock-and-roll.

The strip of Homer Fink's shoelace was in my hand while I was considering all these things. Staring at it, studying the pattern of the separation, I got to thinking about Homer again. It seemed I had been writing Homer's obituary in my mind. Although I wasn't as much for visitations of the spirits and gods as Homer was, this made me very uncomfortable.

I wondered if perhaps Homer had fallen and been fatally injured. That seemed unlikely. But the mood persisted and I couldn't help but feel that something sad—perhaps even tragic—had happened to my friend Homer Fink.

It was true he had done all these things for so many of us. But what had we done for him? I could understand Homer feeling betrayed by all of us. Hadn't we failed him in our determination to achieve the ideal? Weren't we too petty and selfish in our thinking?

And finally—hadn't Homer suspected all along that he would lose the election? Did he feel unwanted and alone? In this melancholy state

—I shuddered to even consider it—was my friend Homer Fink moved to kill himself?

"Homer. Homer Fink. It's me, Richard. *Amo. Amas. Amamos,* Homer," I screamed at the top of my voice.

I rushed down the hill and searched the wooded area adjacent to the falls. Finding no clue of Homer there, I dashed to the field leading to the mansion house and finally ran to the zoo. I moved from the elephant house to the lion's den, from the bird cages to the camel enclosure calling, "Homer-rrr. Homer-rr Fink-kkk. *Amo. Amas. Amamus.* Homer."

When I returned to the hill there was a pounding in my temples and I could feel a trickle of sweat on my upper lip. I remembered Homer telling me, "I'll be on Pan's hill." For all his indifference to the details of appearance and routine, I was positive Homer would not forget this appointment.

I was just beginning to think—to think, as Homer had insisted all along we should. And the thought that came to my mind was—we have destroyed him. He was too good, too pure, too honest, and we were unable to face him—for in facing him we had to face ourselves. And so we destroyed him, erased him from the face of the earth. It was probably the most dramatic moment I had ever made up all by myself. I wasn't enjoying it one bit.

It was then that I heard a dog bark. Looking down from the summit of the hill, I saw the shepherd and his sheep coming around the turn of the woods. Argus was chasing a stray lamb, barking at his heels and forcing him back to the herd.

The shepherd was piping a tune on a great wooden flute and by his side I saw Homer Fink, jumping and skipping and clicking his heels together in his uncoordinated way.

There were tears in my eyes and I swallowed hard when I spoke to him. "Sorry, Homer, but you lost."

"Nick, this is my best friend, Richard Sanders," said Homer Fink. "We're classmates at P.S. 79. Perhaps you remember him from the assembly."

Nick held the pipe with one hand and extended the other to greet me.

"The spirit of Pan is in him," said Homer. "Why else would we find a shepherd in Druid Hill Park?"

"Because I no like work m'brother's res'rant," said the spirit of Pan. "And the taste of sheep's milk, she's O.K."

"Stick with him and you'll learn how to milk a sheep," said Homer.

We followed the flow of the falls until we came to a small house overlooking a grassy field. A man was there whom I recognized as the one

Homer had called "Silenus." The shepherd put down his pipe and wiped his sleeve across his lips. He called, "Hey, Tony, put downa bottle, we'se home." The shepherd was piping again as we started to the house. Argus was barking and the sheep were moving in line.

"Sorry about the news, Homer," I said. "If it makes you feel any better you only lost by one vote." Homer smiled softly and then I asked, "Whom did you vote for anyway?"

"The best man," said Homer Fink. "The beginning of knowledge is to know your own limitations."

Silenus was coming to greet us. He had a jug in one hand, a hunk of cheese in the other. "Ahooey, mates," he called. "Steady as you go. We're short of spirits but high on produce."

Homer stumbled, and Argus deserted the sheep and started barking at his heels.

Homer Fink bent down to fasten the broken lace. He tied a small knot. "How's that, Richard?" he said standing. With his thumb and forefinger he made an "O" for onward.

"It's a beginning, Homer," I said. And Homer Fink said, "Did I ever tell you about the American naturalist Henry Thoreau? Now he thought . . ."

I listened a while and then I said, "Say, Homer, suppose you called Patty Esposito or Elaine Steigmar. We could double-date on Saturday."